Coping
with
Bereavement

W. Keith
Hafer, J.D., Ph.D.

Coping
with
Bereavement

Surviving
the Trauma
of Death or Divorce

First Printing: May, 1999

International Standard Book Number
0-88290-663-1

Horizon Publishers' Catalog and Order Number
1253

Printed and distributed
in the United States of America by

 Horizon Publishers
& Distributors, Incorporated

Mailing Address:
P.O. Box 490
Bountiful, Utah 84011-0490

Street Address:
50 South 500 West
Bountiful, Utah 84010

Local Phone: (801) 295-9451
WATS (toll free): 1 (800) 453-0812
FAX: (801) 295-0196

E-mail: horizonp@burgoyne.com
Internet: http://www.horizonpublishers.com

Dedication

This book is dedicated
to all men and women
who suffer bereavement,
and to their children,
whose lives are always changed,
and sometimes shattered,
by the loss of a parent
through death or divorce.

—W. Keith Hafer

Acknowledgments

I wish to give thanks to my wife and counseling partner, Joyce Pennington Hafer, R.N., Ph.D., for her assistance in the preparation of this work. Her support has included the sharing of a judgment stemming from her training and experience and the wisdom flowing from her heart. Without her contribution my effort would have been much less effective than it may be, and my insights would have remained the unilateral conclusions of the masculine mind, denied the balance of feminine understanding.

Appreciation is also expressed to Duane S. Crowther, president of Horizon Publishers, who edited and prepared my revised manuscript for publication, and to the production staff at Horizon who typeset the book, designed its attractive cover, and reintroduced the book to the marketplace with vigorous enthusiasm!

Contents

Part I
Coping with the Death of a Loved One

Part II
Coping with the Loss of a Loved One Through Divorce

Foreword

This book speaks of bereavement—the deep sorrow that comes from the loss of a loved one—from two causes: death and divorce.

Since this book was first published in 1981, the rules of law and social custom that govern matrimony have undergone numerous changes. These changes reflect the growing emancipation of women—from homemaker to bread winner, and from dependent to partner. These changes also include divorce laws, which have emerged from the constraint of "till death do us part" to the concept of "no-fault" separation.

At that time, the new sexual freedoms that were unknown to former generations had changed between men and women, and 50% of all marriages ended in divorce. This wholesale severance of marital ties produced a new level of emotional and psychological stress, and bereavement from the loss of a marriage partner kept pace with the rise in divorce.

Today, almost two decades later, the divorce rate has fallen to 20.6%, but it is heavily skewed by a significant increase in couples who elect to live together without the sanction of law or church, and who end such relationships at will. But such relationships are no longer terminated without possible financial obligations, as "palimony" or post-relationship support for a long-term partner is viewed favorably by the courts in a growing number of states.

As an extension of this behavior, it is no longer uncommon for children to be born illegitimately to such couples, or to single mothers who choose to raise them without the influence of a male parent. We have become a society in which personal desire dominates the moral climate and affects the foundation of matrimony.

As a result of these behavioral changes, bereavement for the loss of a marriage partner through divorce has been extended to the bereavement of separation from an unmarried live-in companion, as well as from a loss of parental influence over the children of unmarried parents.

Where any level of commitment has existed between such partners, the pain of separation can be compounded by feelings of guilt and loss of moral direction. And for men and women raised in the church, bereavement takes on a new dimension that can be alleviated only by a reassessment of moral values and a return to a pattern of living that honors the restraints of an ordered society.

In recognition of the profound changes that have come about in social and domestic behavior, the second edition of this book attempts to provide expanded guidelines for recovery from both death and divorce—the two major causes of bereavement that reflect today's social climate, and for recovery from the needs that new social climate imposes on the bereaved. That it may assist in bringing about a renewal of hope and balance in the lives of its readers is the ardent prayer of the author.

In an effort to regenerate the strength that flows from a partnership with the Spirit of God, this book places emphasis on the opportunity for all men and women to use this strength to heal the wounds of loss. Without recognition and acceptance of this power, the path to recovery can be longer and more difficult, and reliance on mental effort alone to bring about healing is a rejection of the true source of all healing.

Introduction

A mong the many ills to which mankind is heir, none is more excruciating than grief, and none is less revealed in science or philosophy.

The seven principal losses, which produce deep stress and grief in man, are:

- Loss of a loved one by death.
- Loss of a loved one by divorce.
- Loss of a treasured friendship.
- Loss of a country (or citizenship) by enemy or political action.
- Loss of a job or vocation.
- Loss of a home or business by economic disaster, fire, or other natural cause.
- Loss of capital that represents a substantial part of one's economic protection.

This book deals with the first two of these grief-causing losses. Each of these losses can produce grief; and when combined in any number, the effect can be a level of grief that is overpowering.

The basic purpose of this book is to provide a review of the problems associated with the loss of a loved one through either death or divorce, and to offer suggestions for coping with the various forms and manifestations of loss.

It is hoped that the many insights about how to overcome the problems which accompany the death of a loved one will provide valuable guidance for those who must face that challenge.

Further, it is hoped that the insights about the far-reaching implications of divorce which this book sets forth will provide an increased incentive to unhappily married couples to commit themselves to an in-depth examination of their marriages, and to seriously consider what divorce could mean to them and their children before they commit to that course of action. By so doing, they may well discover that repairing their marriages is a far more desirable solution than the traumatic and far reaching acts of separation and divorce.

Where divorce already has occurred, the need and methods for attaining self-fulfillment are reviewed. In the process of self-examination, it is hoped that those for whom divorce seems to be the only practical solution can attain a new level of self-understanding. This should make it possible to survive divorce with an expanded self-identity, and with a new determination to use divorce as a growth experience from which can come new strengths and an expanded life in the years that follow the ending of a marriage.

Part I

Coping with the Death of a Loved One

1
The Pain of
Losing a Family Member

The Purpose of This Book

In *Much Ado About Nothing*, William Shakespeare wrote, "Every man can handle grief but he that has it." And if it is *your* grief with which you suddenly are dealing, you may find yourself devastated beyond measure, bereft of all that has central meaning in your life, and deaf to the sinuous claims of all well-wishers that "it will pass."

Of course, the well-wishers are right. Your grief will, in time, abate. But the time of healing may be measured in years rather than months, and may be the most agonizing experience you will ever encounter in your lifetime.

The purpose of this book is to make your time of grieving shorter and your return to a balanced life quicker. In the process of offering aids to healing, it also can provide important insights to help you in your knowledge of the dynamics of grief—for if you are able to understand not only *what* is happening to you, but *why* it is happening, and that *it happens to all* who are bereaved, you will be better able to deal with the pain of grief and overcome it.

The Chronological Path of the Grieving Process

In writing about the loss of a beloved person which produces grief, it should be stated in the beginning that extensive field research by the author—as well as a careful review of the professional literature concerning the bereavements of death and divorce—indicates that there is little discernible difference in the potential symptoms, depth, or duration of grief which each form of loss can bring. In addition, the actual quality and extent of the grief that accompanies the loss of a mate by physical death, as well as from the death of a marriage, inevitably is responsive to the same seven factors listed later in this chapter.

For this reason, although the grief of death, as separate from the grief of divorce, will be dealt with in different chapters (in the hope that this separation will be useful to those readers who suffer from only one form of these two bereavements), you will find occasional cross-references in this book, which result from the commonality of the symptoms of each form of loss.

Because of the psychological trauma associated with the loss of a loved one, grief can be classified as a mental illness. It also can be potentially disturbing to physical functions to such a degree that can be as disabling as a serious physical injury. To better understand grief, it may help to perceive it as a reactive depression, or separation anxiety, which is *part of a process*, rather than a state. And assuming that the loss of a partner by death or divorce is not desired, the process of grieving usually will follow this chronological path:

1. *Denial of loss* ("He can't be gone!")
2. *Realization of loss* ("Oh, God, it's true. He's gone forever!")
3. *Feelings of abandonment, alarm, and anxiety* ("Dear God, how will I ever make it alone?")
4. *Despair* (crying, physical numbness, mental confusion, and indecisiveness)
5. *Restlessness* (anxiety, insomnia, loss of appetite, irritability, loss of self-control, and a wandering mind)

6. *Anger* ("Why did he have to die? Why didn't he take better care of himself? I gave him the best years of my life! Now what do I do?")
7. *Guilt* ("I should have taken better care of him. It's my fault he got sick!")
8. *Feelings of loss of self, or total emptiness* ("Half of me is gone forever!")
9. *Longing* (the dull ache that won't go away, even when you are with others)
10. *Identification with your lost partner* (by assuming some of his traits, attitudes, and mannerisms)
11. *Profound depression* ("I just want to die!")
12. *Pathological aspects* (a myriad of minor aches and ailments and a marked tendency toward hypochondria: "Who will take care of me now?")
13. *Voluntary return to society*
14. *The diminishment of grief symptoms, and the beginning of full recovery*

How Long Does Grieving Last?

The answer to this question depends on many factors, the principal ones being these:

1. The degree of your attachment or love for your lost partner.
2. The period of psychological preparation for your loss, if any.
3. Your age and general health at the time of bereavement.
4. Your financial security when bereavement occurs.
5. Your vocational satisfaction and rewards at the time of bereavement.
6. The extent of your supportive family network.
7. The presence and affection of a close circle of friends to help you cope.

Grief begins at the time of loss and builds slowly as recognition of loss assumes reality. In extreme cases, shallow grief can be dissipated in a period of weeks, while deep grief can remain for an unnumbered period of years. *Wow* .

Two examples from the author's files show this contrast: a widow who did her husband's every bidding, subordinating her life to his for forty years, on his death heaved a sigh of relief and began for the first time to live for herself. She honored and loved her husband's memory, but savored to the fullest her newly found freedom. At the other extreme, a man who lost his wife to his next-door neighbor still retained every symptom of deep bereavement twenty-seven years later.

The Physical Aspects of Grief

Like the emotional pain of loss, the physical manifestations of loss can take a myriad of forms. However, most research shows seven symptoms to be most common among people in a state of bereavement, as follows:

1. Waves of physical distress marked by crying, sobbing, and sometimes by screaming.

2. Closing up of the throat muscles, making swallowing uncomfortable.

3. A feeling of choking and loss of breath.

4. Heavy and repeated sighing.

5. An empty feeling in the abdomen.

6. Lack of muscle power; muscle aches and pains.

7. A feeling of extreme tension, as if you're going to explode inside.

Like the duration of grief, its physical manifestations are responsive to the same seven factors that modify its length of term.

Differences in the Grief Perception of Men and Women

Although loss of a loved one is equally painful for both sexes, notable differences in bereavement typically are felt by men than are felt by women:

- In both death and divorce, men typically speak of having lost a part of themselves. Women tend to feel they have been deserted.
- Women tend to find work an antidote to sorrow. In contrast, having been more sustained in their work drive by their wives, men who suddenly are alone in life often experience a noticeable diminishment in their ability to concentrate on their work.
- Men, tending to be more realistic than women, generally have more self-control in bereavement.
- Men tend to have more guilt feelings about death or divorce than women, but lose them sooner.
- Men usually have less personal concern than women about mental breakdowns caused by grief.
- In loss by death, men are less disturbed by funerals than women, and tend to be more critical of undertakers and funeral expenses.
- In loss by divorce or death, men have less concern about finances (as they generally have more control over them) than women.
- In divorce bereavement, men who do not receive custody of children tend to grieve longer than women, and to experience a deeper sense of loss.
- In loss by death, men are prone to recover emotionally sooner than women.
- When a partnership ends by death or divorce, men generally remarry sooner than women.
- Men miss the sexual side of marriage more than women, and usually are quicker to replace it in their lives.

- Men are less fatalistic about loss than women, and tend to be less prone to blame themselves for the loss.

No matter what the dynamics of the loss of a partner, it can be the most shattering event you ever will experience. And because death is the ultimate end of living, and the unwanted end of a committed relationship, it can produce a feeling of profound, ego-shattering rejection. The potential loss of a partner should be faced by all who give their hearts to another.

Concerning death, man has yet to find a way to avoid the ultimate deterioration of the body. For this reason, psychological preparation for death should begin in childhood. If one believes in the resurrection and the immortality of the soul, an acceptance of death as the doorway to a new and fuller life can be a source of supreme comfort. And if one believes that there is no life after death, it can be viewed as a welcome surcease at last from the pain of living.

Regardless of one's view concerning death, a useful goal of society well could be the open recognition of the inevitability that our life form must one day end, and a willingness to share death as an experience common to us all. From such sharing could come new strengths for man to pay death's debt without demur.

2
Loss by Death:
How to Surmount It

The Statistics of Widowhood

The statistics of widowhood are shocking. Today there are more than 29 million widows in the United States,[1] with 700,000 more joining their ranks each year. Of this number, only 16,000 will remarry in any one year, with the chances of remarriage decreasing as the age of the widow increases.

The unpleasant odds are that three out of every four wives will be widowed, with their loss occurring between the ages of fifty and seventy. Most of these widows will suffer a level of bereavement that will vary from painful to acute, and which will last from twelve to twenty-four months or longer, depending on the depth of emotional attachment the widow had to her husband, and the length of time involved in the forewarning of death—the longer the warning, the less acute the bereavement is likely to be.

Because of the large number of women who already are widows, and the even greater number who one day will be faced with widowhood, it is hoped that this chapter will provide insights to help alleviate the stress of past, present, and future widows.

---

[1] Statistical Abstract of the U.S., 1997.

Social Support

The word *widow* means "empty" in Sanskrit, and it best describes the physical state of most women who have lost their mates. This feeling of emptiness must be filled before recovery from your loss can take place. And as it can only be filled with human contact, it is important to know what social support you can expect to receive in your state of grief.

As a widow, you can be sure of receiving certain preferred treatment by society in general. Although this treatment may not be supportive enough to counterbalance your grief, it *will* be important to you in your recovery from bereavement.

First, you will receive the full respect and moral support of your social group and of society in general, and you will find friends and strangers alike eager to touch your hand in comfort and encouragement. Prominent among your comforters will be family members, neighbors, members of your church, and the religious leaders who assist you in your search for God. You also will be accorded the respectful attention and good wishes of all members of your community with whom you come in periodic contact; you will receive their tender expressions of sorrow and vague offers of help "of any kind." And all of this helps with the social aspects of your grief, reinforcing your knowledge that society in general approves of your blameless state of widowhood.

Value of a different kind will accrue to you as a widow from the attitudes of special courts that have been designed for the express purpose of protecting widows and their issue from those who would prey on them in their extremity. This too is comforting and provides valuable support.

Social Expectations

In exchange for the unrestrained approval of society and the church, and the assiduous protection of the courts, you will be expected to conform to certain standards of conduct which are rooted in ancient social custom, and which today can be perceived by some as onerous and restrictive.

Among the public acts expected of you as a widow will be some sort of ceremonial leave-taking of your husband, such as a funeral, a graveside service, or commemorative cremation service; the arranging of a brief but suitable eulogy to sum up the public virtues of your late mate, and the acceptance of flowers or other gifts in tribute to his memory. In some communities and in some cultures, you also will be expected to wear black or dark clothing for a suitable period of time, and to observe sober and decorous conduct in public places.

When the period following death—which has just been described—is ended, and you have made obeisance to all of the social requirements, what comes next? What are the pitfalls of your new widowhood, and how can you avoid them? To help you recognize and deal with the principal problems you can expect to encounter as a widow, many of them are reviewed below by type.

Social Trials For Widows

Right after your husband died, all your friends rallied around, giving you support without limit. Although you were too overcome by sorrow to fully appreciate their condolences and solicitude, the general idea broke through your grief that the world that had been your social microcosm was solidly behind you, and you derived great comfort from the knowledge that nothing had changed except the death of your mate. Don't you believe it! *Everything* has changed, as you will learn.

First off, you will find that our society is inflexibly geared to the dyadic approach, or pairing. If your children are grown and leading separate lives, or if you have no children, there is no natural place for you in the social structure; the regular

social invitations you exchanged with other couples will slowly dwindle down, then quietly disappear.

This is not to say that you will be socially ostracized. Far
from it. If you are a churchgoer you will find your Sunday
greetings as warm as ever, and your departure from old friends
and acquaintances equally effusive, with smiling requests
such as "Let's get together soon, dear!" But "soon" has a way
of never coming.

Barely before your partner's remains have found their last
resting place you will be inundated with offers of "help" from
the husbands of your women friends and neighbors. Slipping
quietly into your kitchen, they will say variations of this: "Call
on me, my dear, for anything you need. Absolutely *anything*.
I admired your husband a lot, and although I know I can't fill
his shoes, just know that I'm available at any time!"

Of course there are friends and neighbors who are concerned with your leaking kitchen sink, or the loose board in
your front steps, or the peeling paint on the north side of your
house, and they truly are the salt of the earth. Unfortunately,
there is a serious shortage of this kind of salt, and the message
sent by your friendly male neighbor was possibly this: "I
know you're going to miss sex with your husband, and I'd be
happy to meet your need in a perfectly discreet way, of course,
seeing as how we're such close neighbors and all." Beware!

Financial Pitfalls

Although the law is zealous in its aim to protect the surviving spouse, the world is filled with fast operators who are
ready and eager to accept the challenge of separating widows
from their dowers as quickly and painlessly as possible.

Unfortunately, many of these sharpshooters have taken on
the coloration of credibility; their fleecing techniques are
legitimate in all but purpose. When faced with an introduction

to such a person, you often will confuse him with an attorney or a banker—for his disguise is the very naturalness of his demeanor, and his offers to help you with your investments (sale of your house, consolidation of your real estate, etc.) are highly legitimate and often follow the recommendation of a third party whom you know and have no reason to distrust.

Unless your husband was a lawyer, a banker, or an accountant who appointed a trusted professional associate to administer his will and oversee his estate, your best bet is to seek an appointment with a senior officer of your bank. Ask him to recommend a successful, ethical, and competent lawyer to whom you can turn for honest and knowledgeable guidance in rebuilding the financial structure of your newly single life.

If your husband had an account with a stock brokerage firm, you will receive an early call from his customers' representative. When he or she calls, take careful note of his or her advice, and ask for a written summary of your husband's account along with a recommendation for its future course. When it is received, take it to your lawyer for review. In the end, you will have to decide whether you want or need high-return, short-run investments, or those of a lower, fixed yield and longer term. You also may have to decide between the risk of stocks over the (relative) security of bonds. But whatever your decision, be alert to any effort to switch your investments from one source to another at frequent intervals. This technique is called "churning," a devious device to generate the maximum amount of sales commission by the multiple turning over of your investments.

Unless your husband was an insurance-company executive, or sales representative, the world of insurance may be a mystery to you. You will do well to seek highly ethical insurance counsel (recommended by your lawyer) before you give serious consideration to any insurance program proposed for your protection. This particularly includes *all* forms of health and disaster (cancer) insurance, many of which are offered by companies operating only marginally within the law.

Should You Move?

If you have inherited real estate, either improved or unimproved, you are fair game for all real estate agents who seek to list your property for sale. To protect yourself, identify and personally call on the president of the local Board of Realtors, and ask him or her to guide you in any real estate transactions that may result from your new status as a widow.

When he or she has collected all relevant facts and carefully analyzed your real estate equities, ask for a summary of your position, along with recommendations for your best plan of action.

If you know any officer of a savings and loan association, your next visit should be to his or her office. If you have no such acquaintance, ask an officer of your bank to recommend such a person and make an appointment to see him or her. In the ensuing meeting, show your realtor's plan to the savings and loan officer and ask the officer's judgment. If it is markedly different from the advice your realtor has offered, seek a third opinion from your lawyer. Then make up your own mind, using the best judgment you can muster to deal with the facts at hand.

If you and your husband have been home owners, and if your children are grown and living under their own roofs, you will receive much advice from well-meaning friends and business counselors to consider selling your home and moving to a "carefree" condominium of smaller size. If your home is mortgage free, one of the arguments advanced for this move will be the opportunity to pay less for a condominium than you will realize from the sale of your house, and it will be pointed out that you can invest the difference in income-producing equities.

Although such advice is sound enough in theory, whether or not it is appropriate for you is a question you should carefully explore. Even if you find the arithmetic attractive and are able to locate a condominium that seems to meet your every need, proceed with great care. Not only are all condominiums not good and/or safe long-term investments—regardless of compelling arithmetic—they seldom are built to afford the level of auditory privacy you have come to expect as a home owner, and you may well find your neighbors' stomach problems less than confidential if their bathrooms happen to be on the opposite side of your walls. Worse than this, unless your building has individual air conditioning and heating units that are properly designed and insulated for quiet operation, you also may find the central duct system an interesting and indiscriminate carrier of private conversations and personal acts.

And perhaps the most offensive of all trials is the possibility that your apartment ceiling may be under the roof where the central air-conditioning system is located. If such should be the case, your life in warm weather will resemble a work shift in a boiler factory, as the condenser(s) switch on and off endlessly.

And if this were not enough to deter you, consider with care two more building features: the floors and the windows. If the building is older, and was built with living comfort rather than quick profit in mind, your floors well may be finished with tile, terrazzo, or parquet—all of which are beautiful to the eye and desirable in the extreme. However, they also are active sound conductors, and if your neighbor in the apartment above you uses area rugs, you will hear every tap of every heel, night and day, over your head.

As for the windows, most modern architects seem to have forgotten that their main purpose was to provide easy passage of cross-ventilated air throughout the living space of each room. As a result, many modern condominiums feature a combination of a few horizontally sliding windows, wall-to-wall sliding doors onto a balcony or terrace, and *no other device* for the passage of air except the ubiquitous and ever noisy air-conditioning equipment.

Even if you can afford the monthly maintenance fee for your condominium—a not inconsiderable sum in many cases—and believe that all of your physical needs for a quiet and comfortable life are met in the condominium of your choice, consider with care the psychological needs that were satisfied so often by digging in your garden, planting your favorite flowers, or just watching the birds wheel and land in your trees, calling their seasonal greetings to each other and to you. Sometimes, for some people, *this* aspect of home ownership more than outweighs any possible convenience or economic advantage of apartment living. You and you alone must be the final judge.

If you live in the last home you shared with your husband, and for personal reasons wish to continue to enjoy this form of housing independence, consider sharing your home with a single and compatible relative or friend, to whom the joys of life in a single-family dwelling might have appeal. Such a solution, when entered into with care and mutual accord, can become one of the most satisfactory and supportive living arrangements you can make. It often results in a new level of contentment and companionship, as well as in better health and longer life.

Social Support Systems

Ideally, you are in a group of widows whose annual incomes from all sources total twenty thousand dollars or more. If so, you are likely to find one or more of the above suggestions to be of practical value. However, if you happen to be one of the 40 percent who live below the so-called poverty level, other suggestions can be helpful to you, as follows:

Check your eligibility for Social Security benefits under your husband's coverage, as well as for Medicare and Medicaid, all part of the federal Old Age Assistance Act, to which every citizen has some form of entitlement. Check your eligibility for food stamps. This form of federal support is not a charity, but a part of a program of social welfare supported by the taxes your husband paid over the years; it is a vested right for all who meet the eligibility requirements.

Many communities, particularly in the Southeast and Southwest, which attract retirees and sun worshippers to warmer climates, have developed elaborate social support systems for widows and widowers, as well as older citizens. However, no matter where you live, be sure to check with your local United Fund office, and with city hall for a list of facilities that may be available at very low cost or no cost at all. Such services often include those that appear in alphabetical order at the end of this chapter.

Typical social services of possible value to widows, which are available in many cities, include:
- Aging advocacy groups
- Blind/visually handicapped services
- Credit and budget counseling
- Crisis intervention centers
- Community human relations services
- Community recreation/culture activities
- Employment assistance
- Extension education opportunities
- Eyeglass provision
- Financial assistance during employment training
- General emergency financial assistance
- Health counseling information
- Job placement and referral

- Job training
- Landlord and tenant rights
- Legal assistance center
- Meals on Wheels for shut-ins
- Neighborly Centers (where one free hot meal is served each day in a social atmosphere, to which those without cars are transported in free buses
- Recreation activities for the handicapped

The Principle Stresses of Widowhood

So far we have dealt largely with the practical side of survival. Now that it is out of the way, the even more important aspect of your inner or psychological life must be examined and reinforced.

If you are a widow who recognizes the fact that most women today outlive their husbands, the chances are high that you will experience a much shorter period of mourning, for the reason that your psyche has been preparing you for an ultimate separation in a way that not only anticipates (and thereby dilutes) grief, but that actually can serve to endow the joy of living with one's mate with a deeper and richer meaning.

However, if you are an average widow who has assiduously avoided thought or conversation about the potential death of your mate, you can expect to share the principal stresses of your new state, which include those appearing below:

- *Loss of social identity as a wife, and acceptance of a lower social identity as a widow.* If you are one who had primarily identified yourself with a husband and children, your sense of loss will be acute and will include your personal identity.
- *A general sense of confusion*, which will be expressed in memory lapses, difficulty in concentrating, and wandering thoughts.

- *Fear about financial security.* Although many widows are well off financially, the majority find themselves with a reduced income, which can be a source of constant stress.
- *Intense and pervasive loneliness.* If your union was one of extreme rapport, you will be lonely for the *person* of your husband. If it was less than idyllic, you will be lonely for a partner.

The Challenge of Depression

Depression usually is a companion of loneliness. If you experience depression, it can produce these symptoms, in varying and fluctuating degrees:

- A feeling of hopelessness and despair.
- Changes in level of physical activity.
- Loss of self-esteem and feelings of self-worth.
- Fear of rejection, which may cause social withdrawal.
- Inordinate sensitivity to the words or actions of others.
- Unexplained irritability.
- Free-floating and often withheld anger.
- Feelings of guilt and self-blame.
- Extreme dependency on others.
- Suicidal feelings or acts.

All of these stresses will be disruptive of your well-being, and as death is the most traumatic of all life changes, a high level of stress—or a combination of many stresses—can result in physical illness: the body's response to shock and its effort to immobilize you while healing takes place.

However, of all the stresses you may experience, none can be more devastating than depression. The following suggestions are offered for coping with the depression that can follow the loss of a loved one:

• Accept your grief and express it. If you feel like crying, cry. It is nature's way of reducing stress. And take time to grieve, for grieving is a vital process in healing.

• If possible, share your feelings with someone you trust. This will help restore your perspective and reduce your feeling of being alone.

• Change your daily routine. This will be of value in freeing up your frozen tensions. If financially possible for you, take a vacation (if you are employed), or a trip (if you don't work). If no one you care for is available to go with you, go alone. Change is healing. And if you are truly open to new friendships, they are sure to follow.

• Engage in some form of physical activity appropriate to your age, such as tennis, swimming, dancing, bicycling, jogging, or just plain walking. And try to do it daily. If none of these activities appeal to you, or are not possible for some reason, join a class in Yoga. Not only will it help to tone up your body and work off tensions, but it can soothe your battered spirit. It also can lead to new friendships, which you need to form.

• Try to find something you can do well, and do it often. This will help rebuild your impaired self-esteem.

• Focus your energy on someone else—perhaps someone who is old or sick or lonely. This will help take your mind off your loss, and will aid you in conquering self-pity.

• Take a good, honest look at your appearance, decide how it might be improved, and set about changing it for the better. This will improve your self-image.

• Get involved in activities with others—anything that takes you out of the house and broadens your horizons and your social contacts. Be open to sharing yourself and your identity with new acquaintances. This will encourage them to share in return, and will plant the seeds of friendship.

• If you have any latent skill or unused training, consider putting it to use vocationally, either full or part time. This will help to rebuild your feeling of independence. It also will augment your income and help reduce any financial pressure you may be feeling.

• If you have no discernible or marketable skills, and married too young to have acquired any significant training, consider returning to school.

• If there are valid reasons why a return to the marketplace or to school is not practical for you—such as physical infirmity or advanced age—consider sharing your home or apartment with another person in similar financial circumstances. This should be a person you like and respect, and with whom you are socially compatible and have interests in common. Having someone to talk with, to shop or travel with, can alleviate your loneliness and reduce any fears you may have about solitary existence. And sharing your living expenses can increase the standard of living for each of you.

• If your depression persists and/or leads you to serious thoughts of self-destruction, seek professional help. This usually can be found in your local community at one or more of the social service agencies that receive their support from public funds. Prominent among such groups are family service agencies and mental health clinics.

• If you have a deep religious orientation, turn to your church and draw on the spiritual meaning it has for you. If you are one who has an unexpressed sense of identity with an infinite Father or Supreme Being, devote twenty minutes or more before breakfast each morning to a time of quiet prayer and meditation, in which you seek to become one with your own spirit and the spirit of the Divine. Like nothing else, the opening yourself to the healing powers of the spirit within can restore you to new and exuberant mental and physical health, and can help to direct you toward your own greatest fulfillment in the years ahead. At the same time, this sense of unity with the spark of God within—sought and found in daily meditation—can reward you with the feeling of having an ever-present and highly personal source of comfort and protection, and can take the bitter edge off your feeling of being alone. It also can endow you with an aura of peace, which will attract to you others whose heavy inner burdens also are being carried alone.

As stated earlier, depression and loneliness usually are companion symptoms in bereavement. Like depression, loneliness can lead to excessive suffering, and can destroy your ability to function in a rational way. Because loneliness is an emotional response common to the bereavements of divorce as well as death, it is covered in some detail in a later chapter. The suggestions offered there for coping with loneliness will be of benefit to all widows (and widowers) who are experiencing this strong and potentially crippling emotion.

Probably because widowers as a group usually have been more dependent on marriage for personal satisfaction than their wives, and usually experience greater difficulty in coping successfully with household management, 50 percent of all widowers will remarry within the first year; and most will enter into subsequent legal unions much sooner than widows. Also, although many of us tend to repeat our mistakes, the second marriage experience for most widowers will be a positive one, benefiting from lessons learned in the first marriage.

Nonetheless, most widowers will experience the same manifestations, if not the same level of bereavement as widows; and men who have lost their wives through death may find the suggestions made to widows in this chapter to be of value.

3
Counsel for Widowed Fathers

Sole custody of minor children by their fathers can be a formidable challenge. It also can be a comfort, in the early stages of bereavement, to share your grief with your child or children, as the giving and receiving of comfort can ease the shattering pain and become the beginning of a mutually supportive, new and different parent-child relationship.

Explaining Mother's Absence

If your children are very young, the first difficulty you will face is explaining "mommy's" disappearance from their lives. Be conscious that young children have no concept of death and will need to hear statements that help them to understand the finality of death. If you are a member of a church or synagogue, ask your bishop, pastor or rabbi for suggestions that conform to your particular beliefs. Do not say things like, "God took mommy," "mommy went to sleep," or "mommy went away." Children are very literal minded and believe your *words* without the ability to understand a deeper meaning. Answer questions honestly, but do not answer what has not been asked. Simplicity is always best when offering explanations to children.

In the early days of your bereavement, family and friends will be available and eager to assist you with the day-to-day needs of you and your children. However, within a few weeks they will return to their own lives and schedules and you will be faced with the need to be both a father and mother to your children.

Acquiring New Homemaking Skills

As overwhelming as this appears, you can learn new ways of managing your time and energy, as well as homemaking skills previously performed by your wife.

If you can afford it, hire a local woman, whom you trust, to be in the home when your children return from school and remain until you arrive in the evening. If this is not possible, investigate after-school care that is available in many elementary schools for working parents. For preschool children, investigate licensed day care centers, but be sure to request letters of recommendation from parents who have used the center.

You also will need to set priorities and develop schedules, a difficult task if your children have become accustomed to total care and service from a "stay at home" mom.

If your wife was employed outside the home, and children had assigned duties within the household, schedules will need only to be modified to meet the new family structure.

Your inclination may be to shield your children from the responsibilities of being part of a single-parent home as they recover from the bereavement of their loss. However, they will recover more quickly, and feel more secure, when they have an active role within the family, and even very young children can be assigned simple chores (pick up toys, put clothes in hamper, etc).

Communicating Effectively with Your Children

Returning your family to an adequate functioning level will take planning and work on your part. Suggestions for beginning appear below:

  1. Encourage your children to talk about their mother. Speaking about her, and reviewing the time of her illness/

accident and death will help them remain emotionally connected with her until they are able to accept their loss and move on.

2. Schedule regular family meetings in which problems are discussed and solutions sought. This meeting should include all children, regardless of age.

3. Develop a list of rules and expectations for your children. Encourage their input. You will find it much easier to enforce rules upon which children have agreed.

4. Develop consequences for any breech of acceptable behavior and be consistent in their execution. Children need to have firm boundaries to feel secure. When rules are enforced by whim, children feel insecure and unsafe.

5. When your children complain, as they will that "Mom always—," or "Mom never—," resist the temptation to feel guilty and give in. An honest and simple response might be, "Yes, and it was wonderful. But Mom is gone, and we must adjust to the life we now have, even though it is not easy."

6. Accept your limitations.

7. Seek the assistance of a female family member, close friend, or church member, to act as a role model and guide for your female children. If none are available, investigate the organization called "Big Sisters/Big Brothers," and ask them to assign a volunteer to spend quality time with your daughter(s).

8. Allow your children to be disappointed. That's a part of life. Any attempt to make their world perfect now will result in sorrow and frustration in later years.

9. Allow your children to be angry. Anger is a normal and healthy response to life's frustrations, especially one as severe as the loss of their mother. Your job is to show them healthy ways to express their anger. Be sympathetic, but try not to become involved in their anger.

10. Encourage open communication. If you can listen to your child's problems, mistakes and frustrations *without judgment*, you will have an opportunity to teach coping skills and values that will aid him or her later in making wise decisions.

11. Listen, really listen to your children! Your complete attention, even for a few minutes a day, will teach you how they think and feel. Ask interested questions about what they tell you, but *don't pry*. Children often have secret feelings which they are not ready to share, and undue probing will gain nothing but negative feelings.

Drawing Nurture from Support Groups

As you face the years ahead, remember that, like your children, you need to be nurtured. You will miss the emotional support of a life partner and may be tempted to place your children in the position of confidant. But do not allow yourself to do this. It will be counterproductive and will elevate them to the level of peer, leaving them with no adult role model. A better choice is to join a support group for single parents or widowers. Many churches offer such groups. Those who are experiencing similar pain and loneliness can be a great help in reestablishing your feelings of wholeness and self-esteem.

Developing a New Love Relationship

As you recover from your loss and begin to look to the future, you will have abundant opportunities for social contact with women who also are alone and lonely. It is wise to move slowly into these new friendships. However, an interest in establishing new relationships is a sign that you are healing and ready to move forward into a new life.

This may be a time of apprehension for your children as they perceive a relationship with any woman as an attempt to "replace" their mother. Should you date? Absolutely, but take care to avoid overt signs of physical affection between you and your female friend in their presence unless, or until, they have come to accept the idea of Dad showing interest in another woman.

Be open and honest with your children about your female friends, but keep your comments simple. "She's a nice lady, I like her," or "Jane and your mom were friends and I enjoy sharing memories with her."

Should you be blessed in developing a loving relationship with a woman, begin to involve your children in outings with the two of you. Do things that they will enjoy, but keep these shared times simple and easy to manage. A trip to the zoo, a game of miniature golf, a board game at home, a rented movie and a shared bowl of popcorn or other snack will offer a level of comfort and an opportunity to be together without the pressure of organizing or being involved in a big event.

If you plan to re-marry, allow time for your children to develop an easy and comfortable relationship with your intended before you announce your plans. When the time comes, sit down with your children and ask their blessing. Listen to their concerns, and recognize their need to be involved in the decision and the wedding plans. In reality, you are not entering marriage as a single person, but as a family.

Blending Two Families into One

If your intended also has children, and you will blend families, involve all the children. It will be complicated and confusing, but in the end will help to bind the family together as a unit. Step-parenting can be one of life's greatest challenges. It also can bring you unexpected rewards in the companionship and affection of an extended family.

Suggestions for coping with issues related to blended families can be found in chapter five of this book.

Part II

Coping with
the Loss
of a Loved One
Through Divorce

4

The Trauma of a Broken Marriage: How to Survive It

I f your form of loss has been the death of a marriage, you can be feeling any or all of the symptoms of the bereavement of physical death, and this chapter is written for you.

Statistics on Divorce

If you have any ethical or religious proscriptions concerning the sanctity and eternal nature of marriage vows, or if you are feeling shameful and socially outcast because your union was severed long before death did you part, perhaps you'll feel better—or at least less like a pariah—if you take a look at the astonishing statistics about divorce that follow:

In 1860 the divorce rate in the United States was .3 per 100. By 1990 it had climbed to 40 divorces for every 100 marriages. In 1996 the rate had dropped to 21 for every 100 marriages,[1] which in part reflect the accelerating increase in informal and unblessed unions.

Forty-seven million Americans have been divorced at some point in their lives; and many of these men and women were psychological victims of multiple divorces.

In addition to the number of divorce actions that continue to be filed, it is estimated that at least one million more couples will resort to separation or desertion each year, and that

---

[1] Statistical Abstract of the U.S., 1997.

an additional one million or more couples will continue to live under the same roof, but be psychologically divorced.

A Greater Public Acceptance of Divorce Today

Today the United States accords a degree of public acceptance of divorce never dreamed of only a few years ago. Proof of this change in our social mores is found in the large number of divorced people who occupy important and highly visible positions. Notable among them are a U.S. President, the wife of a former U.S. President, a former U.S. Vice-President and his wife, U.S. Supreme Court justices (one of whom was multiply married while on the bench), governors of states, U.S. senators and representatives, university presidents, a growing number of clergymen, a wide assortment of men and women who have achieved notable success in business and the professions, and even England's Prince of Wales. In short, by the last decade of the twentieth century, divorce has become commonplace and acceptable as a means to end legally sanctioned relationships that are no longer tenable; and your problems as a divorced person are shared by men and women everywhere, at all socioeconomic levels and in all vocations.

Regardless of economic or social position, the death of a marriage can have a marked effect on friendships and associations that were shared, causing feelings of bereavement for the loss of those relationships as well.

The Symptoms of Divorce Bereavement

As stated in the first chapter, the loss of a partner by divorce can produce many or all of the same symptoms—and to the same depth and for an equal duration—as a loss by death.

The reasons for this are obvious: divorce, like death, results in an extensive reorganization of one's life, life-style, and economics. It nearly always has a profound impact on one's own self-concept and relationship with others. In addition, if there are children, divorce changes the course of life for an entire family unit.

In 1979, an American physician named R. H. Rahe revealed the results of a detailed study of crises that occur in the lives of most of us at one time or another. In so doing, Dr. Rahe developed a scale of intensity of stress resulting from the most common life events, which revealed that people rate intensity of stress on a scale of 1 to 100 as follows:

Death of a spouse	100
Divorce	73
Marital separation	65

In short, the pain associated with the loss of a partner, by any means, is one of the most stressful events you can ever experience. And although there is no way you can avoid this stress, it may be of value to review for you the symptoms most frequently encountered among divorced people. Thus, for whatever psychological value it may have for you, you will know that your suffering is a common agony experienced by most others who are divorced, in the following order:

1. Anxiety/fear
2. Sadness/regret
3. Anger/frustration
4. Insecurity
5. Loneliness
6. Guilt
7. Longing

In addition to these most-common symptoms of divorce, others frequently reported are found in the following statements of recently divorced people:

"I'm shaky, scared, afraid of the dark."

"I have violent mood swings."

"I have lots of colds, sore throats, and other minor ailments I never had before."

"I feel disconnected."

"I miss the predictability and the continuity of marriage."

"There's a void in my life, an emptiness, where my mate's imprint once was."

"There's an ache that won't go away."

"I can't sleep; I need someone to share my life!"

"I feel so alone."

"I feel rejected, unwanted, and lost."

"I truly dread holidays—any holiday, especially Christmas!"

"I need to be needed again."

If the pain reported by others is the pain you are feeling, know that there is hope. For although you can never forget the high moments of joy you shared with your mate, and the exhilaration of being part of a whole social unit, time is nature's greatest healer; in time, your pain will abate and your anguish fade. Until that time has come for you, however, there are supports you can turn to, aids you can use to relieve your stress. They are dealt with below.

Overcoming Fear and Anxiety

First, we will take a look at *anxiety* and *fear*. Opposite sides of the same coin, both are responses to things over which you have limited or no control—a characteristic of divorce. For even in an amicable ending of a marriage, you are setting forth on uncharted seas, and all things unknown hold within them the threat of disaster. When we can clearly see the future—no matter how black it may be—we are able to pre-pare psychologically to meet it. But when the future is obscured from us, we are inclined to invest it with unnamed threats and perils. This is especially true when our defenses are down and we are drained of our reserve emotional strength. Therefore, the best and quickest way to combat your anxiety or fear is to bring it out into the open and try to analyze it. To help you do this, please turn to the end of this chapter and fill in your answers on the *Fear Questionnaire*, p. 59. When you have finished, study your answers to see if they have given you any insight about this emotion as it affects you. Then turn back here to the text and continue reading.

There is no way to predict what responses you have made to these five questions, but there is one certainty about your answers: they have helped you to identify your fears and to determine whether they are physical or emotional, real or imagined. And they also have helped you to face what it is you fear. Once faced, fear will not necessarily disappear, but it will lose some of its power to immobilize you. You can then begin the necessary task of learning to live with and accept your fears for what they are, while doing everything in your power to remove their cause.

Overcoming Regret and Sadness

Now, let's take a closer look at *sadness* and *regret*. If you are experiencing either of these feelings, the chances are high that you were not the moving party in your divorce action, and that it came as a shock to you. Where such is the case, there has been time for your partner to adjust to a loss which he or she was planning to bring about. Even though the instigators of divorce often feel the symptoms of bereavement, the depth and duration of their symptoms generally are less severe, for they were able to begin earlier the psychological process of withdrawal from a marriage that must precede any recovery from the feeling of loss.

Therefore, your own first task in coping with sadness and regret is this: face the fact that your marriage has ended, and build from there. Until you are able to do this, it's all uphill. But once faced, acknowledged, and accepted for what it is—a broken life—the worst is over, and the healing process can begin.

In taking this first and perhaps most terrifying step toward your psychological recovery, you have removed its greatest power to hurt you. You have brought yourself to a point of objectivity from which you can begin to release the pain and sorrow related to a past that, for you, must be forever ended.

In the process of letting go of this sorrow and regret, you will find the need to cry, perhaps to scream and beat your hands against the wall. Follow this impulse whenever it appears, for crying is nature's way of cleansing and healing. If you have friends who are prone to say, "Don't cry; it'll be OK," don't heed their well-meaning counsel—for it will not, it can never be OK for you until you are able to cry as often and as much as your heart needs.

Overcoming Frustration and Anger

And now we come to *anger* and *frustration*. Perhaps you are experiencing neither one of these feelings. If so, you are one of the lucky (or sainted) ones, in whose heart anger never grows. But if you are like most of us, you are feeling angry and hurt, and your level of frustration is nearly boundless, for you gave your life into the keeping of another, and your trust has been betrayed.

In overcoming anger, you are truly cleansing your soul, for anger is a spirit poison that can lead to devastating physical manifestations. There has been at least one well-trained and long-experienced psychiatrist who has seen in anger and frustration the seeds of cancer. Thus, your need to break the bonds of anger could not be greater.

In your effort to accomplish this difficult task, you will be required to face the anger of bereavement for what it is: the dark side of your own ego, for it is the impairment of your self-image that is involved with anger. What your mind is really telling you here is not so much that you hurt as that you have been deserted and left alone, to live or die in your own despair.

So again, as in coping with sadness, in dealing with your anger you will be required to face the fact of your rejection. If you are wiser and stronger than most, you will be concerned not only with losing anger, but with understanding the causal factors involved in your rejection. By this understanding, you will acquire the strength and purpose to bring about modifications in those personality factors that led to your desertion. In this way alone you can at last assure yourself of a happiness to come, of which you were not before capable.

If the strength required to accomplish such a metamorphosis is not yours to command, your insight into the real cause of your anger can in time help it to dissolve, and can pave the way to a renewed self-image with which you can live in harmony and peace.

Overcoming Insecurity

As for the *insecurity* you may be feeling, if its level is high, the chances are that it reflects the change in your financial situation that divorce has brought about. If this is the case, you will be required to accept your circumstances as they are now, while you work in all possible ways to improve your condition. In the process of coping with your feelings of financial (and physical) insecurity, it will be helpful to accept the fact as it is: your life has changed in every aspect. And although such acceptance will not of itself increase your security, it will release for your use the psychic energy you will need to rebuild your life in ways that provide the protection you require.

In working toward this goal, it is important that you understand the psychological dynamics involved. Before, the fact and feeling of your security was drawn from your dependence on another; now it rests largely upon you and you alone. The only answer to your heart's question, "Can I make it on my own?" must be a resounding "Yes, I can!"

A distillation of thousands of years of philosophy concerned with positive thinking shows us that anything man can imagine, he can bring to be. We have abundant proof of this in space capsules that transport men to and return them from other planets, in microsurgery, and in the economic and political recovery from total chaos of countries vanquished in armed conflict a few short years ago. Therefore, know in your heart that whatever level of security you wish to attain—without limitation—can and will be yours if you can determine what goals you wish to strive for, and then fix them clearly in your mind as being capable of attainment in the short, intermediate, or long term.

The very process of choosing your goals, and setting them to timetables designed to bring you security in a series of progressions, is the first and most important step. Take it, and you are on your way to building a life based on your own strengths, which may bend but never bow to the slings and arrows of outrageous fortune, no matter how painful they may once more become.

Overcoming Loneliness

Of all the agonies of bereavement, none is more pervasive than loneliness. It is the fear of being alone that drives many to marry unwisely and in haste. Having done so, it is this same fear that holds many unhappy marriages together in a life of mutual neurotic dependency on the physical presence of each other.   *Not me.*

Thus, when the physical separation of divorce comes to those who were victims of the fear of loneliness, it can be devastating beyond measure, and it can destroy life. Therefore, if loneliness is one of the crosses you bear, take comfort in the knowledge that there are social techniques to combat it, and psychological disciplines which can help you to overcome it.

But first let's examine for a moment such a small but painful fear as being afraid of the dark, which so many bereaved people experience. This particular fear is always with us, waiting to be released by its sister fear of being alone—for fear of darkness is man's inheritance from simian ancestors (if you believe in evolution), or from our soul's intuition of the darkness that opposes light (if you believe in the divine creation of man and the constant challenge by the forces of evil, or darkness). If this particular fear is a part of your loneliness, accept it as a natural manifestation, and combat it in the only practical way: keep a light or lights burning at night in places where fear, for you, lurks most ominously.

On the social side, the first canon in overcoming loneliness is this: make friends—for they are the only fabric in which loneliness can be smothered. To make a friend, it is first necessary that you be open to friendship, willing and eager to give something of yourself in the process. It is only through this giving that true friendship, the supportive level of friendship that you need, can grow.

To make friends it is, of course, necessary that you go where there are people. It also is necessary that you select those places where people with whom you have the greatest compatibility can be found. If your interest lies in sports, or body culture, or physical control, a neighborhood or civic tennis court or swimming pool, or a Yoga class, can be a good place to start.

If dancing turns you on, most communities offer some facility where single dancers can meet others who seek dancing partners. If this is not true where you live, perhaps a community college offers classes in ballroom, square, or western dancing; and this is a good first option. If you happen to have adequate means, or are willing to make an investment dispro- portionate to the size of your purse, there are private dancing schools where you are sure to meet other lonely people whose needs and interests are similar to your own.

If you have a good singing voice, or even experience joy in singing off-key, nearly every church of any size will welcome you to its choir, and the time of practice with other members can open new social horizons for you, as well as occupy your lonely hours.

If none of these activities appeal to you, or if there is some reason why they are not possible for you, many churches in all communities have singles' groups which meet periodically. There you can enjoy the fellowship of socializing that must precede any relationship that can be of real consequence to you.

If you happen to be a divorced person with young children who make it difficult for you to seek social avenues of friend- ship, contact the *Parents Without Partners* group in your com- munity. There you are sure to find others who share one or more of the problems of living alone that plague you, includ- ing loneliness.

In addition to these suggestions for overcoming loneliness by exposing yourself to social contacts with other people who may be alone, you very likely can supply ideas of your own which will bring you in touch with social groups related to your interests.

Among the psychological aids that can be of value in com- bating loneliness is a thoughtful assessment of your own feel- ings about this emotion. You can make this assessment by answering the few questions about yourself that appear at the end of this chapter in the *Loneliness Questionnaire* on page 60. As in the use of the *Fear Questionnaire*, please answer the questions with care, then study them to see what insights you may have derived from this exercise. After you have considered your answers and their possible meaning to you, please turn back to the text and continue reading.

Assuming that you have answered the questions honestly and with objectivity, can you see a pattern of loneliness emerging? If there is a pattern, or profile of your loneliness, examine it carefully to see how it can be combatted.

For example, if you are most lonely at night, arrange with a friend or relation with whom you have rapport for a telephone conversation as close as possible to the time of peak loneliness, to which you can look forward each evening. This conversation does not have to be structured or long. Its purpose is only to reaffirm for you that you are not really a solitary soul, functioning in a void of loneliness, but instead are one of billions of human entities, all functioning alone as extensions of one Supreme Being, of whom you are an integral part. *good idea.* *Daily Michelle*

If weekends or holidays are your worst times for loneliness, you are manifesting highly normal symptoms of bereavement. You can use this knowledge to seek reciprocal liaisons with others who live alone? Being together at prearranged times can be as therapeutic for them as it is for you. *get involved*

You also can try to fill up your most empty days with a schedule of events in which you will participate with others, such as church services; choir practices; amateur theater rehearsals; sports activities; visits to museums, art galleries, or musical events; movies; plays; walks; window-shopping expeditions; or any one or more of dozens of activities that will involve you with others. *Love (F!)*

If holidays are your darkest times, chances are that Christmas will head the list of days on which you feel most alone—for the earliest and most pleasurable memories for most of us are associated with Christmases we have shared with those we loved, who loved us. Therefore, if a lonely Christmas looms ahead for you, here are a few suggestions that may help:

If you have nowhere to go on Christmas, and no one to be with, invite someone to join you in your own celebration. If you are a stranger to your community, or if you do not know anyone you believe might be unattached on Christmas, reveal your need to as many clergymen as it takes to produce a suitable nomination of one to whom your invitation could have meaning. In so doing, the chances also are high that you yourself will receive an invitation to share that holiday's festivities with a family that is reaching out to someone like you.

If all else fails in your efforts to put together or join a joyous Christmas celebration, consider visiting a shut-in or a lonely invalid, whose name you can obtain from your local home health care service or from your church.

If your financial resources are not limited, and Christmas and the attendant holidays are a time of trial for you, invite a friend to take a cruise at your expense; or take one alone—for you are bound to meet others on board your ship who have taken the same cruise for the same reasons of loneliness.

If loneliness for you means a special memory, try facing the memory head-on, giving it as many hours of your time as required for a thorough review. If your first honest effort to let your mind become saturated with this memory is not successful, keep trying—for it is the fragmented, often-avoided recollections that can plague you indefinitely until they are faced for what they are: images from your past, not restrictions on your future.

In sum, to be lonely is to be socially disoriented. Therefore, you may wish to consider the surest cure for loneliness: become involved in an endeavor designed to help others to ameliorate the trials of living. If you are not sure how and where to make contact with groups devoted to public service on a one-to-one basis, contact your clergyman or the minister of any church, or your United Fund office. Let them know what skills or interests you are willing to share with others, and the first and strongest link in the chain which can bind you to the human race will have been forged. You will be on your way out of the land where each man is an island, to a place where every man's needs are every man's concern.

If you have always been lonely, or if loneliness in your bereavement is pervasive and stays with you all the time, or if your loneliness sometimes leads you to thoughts of self-destruction, you are in need of professional help. To arrange for counseling geared to your ability to pay, contact your local family service agency or mental health clinic.

Overcoming Guilt

If you are the one who brought your marriage to an end, for reasons which, to you, had high validity, your former partner will be feeling guilt. But so will you. For no matter what the justification for the severance of your legal ties, you will devote countless hours to second-guessing, to agonizing over the limitless number of *what if's* that come to your mind. And although this response is to be expected as the result of a broken marriage, there is little psychological profit in it for you.

If you happen to be the partner who was an unwilling party to a divorce action, the guilt you are feeling will deal with the omissions and commissions that caused your mate to wish to end your union, and your *what if's* can be an endless chain, interwoven with *if only's*.

In each case (the aggrieved and the aggrievor), the guilt you feel will be a part of the grieving process. Until it has been examined and expressed, your healing cannot be complete. Therefore, accept your guilt, deserved or undeserved, and know that it should begin to fade away with the memories of the things you did (or did not do), or the things you said (or did not say).

If an honest examination of your guilt feelings leads you to see them as not completely rational or deserved, your time of holding guilt will be lessened. On the contrary, if your assessment of blame justifies an intense feeling of guilt, you can be in for some rough times until you reorder your life in a way that balances out the guilt. To do this, it will be necessary for you to draw from your guilt a pattern, or list, of personality and character manifestations that caused you to act (or not act) as you did. Possessed of this insight into yourself, you can begin the arduous task of modifying the behavior that led to your divorce.

As your efforts at behavior modification begin to show results, your guilt will give way to growing self-respect. You can begin to look forward with hope to a new life—perhaps with another partner, perhaps alone. Your efforts to subdue the personal characteristics you find adverse, and emphasize those you perceive as admirable, can lead you to greater happiness in your personal relationships and earlier fulfillment in your chosen work.

If the level of your guilt is extremely high, if your objective assessment of the conduct that caused it leads you to see your guilt as justified, and if your efforts at behavior modification do not bear fruit, you will do well to consider seeking help from your local family service or mental health agency. There you will find professional counselors who are able to assist you in understanding the dynamics of your behavior, toward the end of changing it as you desire.

Overcoming Longing

Longing is best defined as a pervasive and free-floating ache that is associated with our deepest emotions. Where reciprocal love has been present in a relationship, longing will exist. It likely will remain, although in muted form and degree, throughout the lifetime of the one who longs—for a heart once freely given remains forever linked with the object which inspired the gift. s→o.

If you are feeling the pangs of longing that attend a heart-breaking loss, try to accept your feelings as a tribute to the integrity of your gift of love. Acknowledge them openly to yourself-and to others, if need be.

Recognized as the lasting imprint of another's life upon your own, longing must be accepted as the price one pays for a truly shared life when the sharing ends. If you believe with Elizabeth Kubler-Ross, M.D., and Raymond A. Moody, M.D., that death is but a passage through a dark tunnel to the glorious light at the end, then know that longing is but the force compelling you once more into the presence of those you loved, who await your successful passage to a form of further and expanded sharing.

Fear Questionnaire

1. What things do you fear most?
   Being Alone, Not having a family.

2. Are these fears valid? Can they actually happen to you?
   Yes _✓_ No ___ Maybe ___

3. If your answer is "maybe," what factors can produce your fear? *No one ever loving me again.*

4. Can you exercise any control over these factors?
   Yes ___ No _✓_

5. If what you fear does happen, what is the worst thing that can result? *Alone for eternity.*

Loneliness Questionnaire

1. At what time of day and week are you most lonely?
   Morning ___ Evening ___ Night _✗_ Week-ends ___

2. Is this loneliness associated with any particular
   memory? Yes _✗_ No _✗_ - *I felt lonely then too.*

3. If there is an association, describe it.
   Big Bed - All alone.

4. If there is no particular association, what triggers your
   loneliness? *Temple - Reminds me I am alone.*

5. Can you think of any way to avoid this trigger?
   Yes ___ No _✗_ .
   If your answer is "yes," how might you avoid it?
   I am not going to avoid the temple.

6. Did you feel lonely as a child?
   Yes ___ No _✗_

7. If your answer is "yes," when did you stop
   feeling lonely? *I started during my marriage*

8. Were you lonely before your marriage?
   Yes ___ No _✗_

9. Were you ever lonely during your marriage?
   Yes _✗_ No ___   *- All the time*

10. If your answer is "yes," in what ways were you lonely,
    and when were you lonely? *I was physically alone
    all day & all night. I lost most of my other associations*

11. What do you fear most about your loneliness?
    It taking over my daily functions.

12. How valid are these fears?
    Always valid ___ Sometimes valid _✗_
    Seldom valid ___

5
Helping the Bereaved Child

Statistics on One-Parent Families

In 1996, one million children under the age of 18 were involved in divorces in the United States of America, and 24% of all children lived in single-parent families. And in 1998 only about half of all children in the U.S. were living with both natural parents.[1]

Thus, if you are among the thirty-eight million, eight hundred and sixty-eight thousand women who head families today, you no longer are a member of a minority group once judged by society as disordered, immature, and immoral. Instead, you are beginning to be seen as the fulcrum in a social process of change. Whereas a single-parent family can and does exist in many still intact marriages, to the detriment of the children involved, a one-parent household that is well ordered can be a better environment for children who have been vicariously involved in the bickering, anger, and abject hatred that existed in a dysfunctional two-parent family.

However, despite the logic of the concept expressed above, the fact remains that children of divorce need special understanding and special help, for a child's heart breaks easily and is especially vulnerable to events over which it has no control. And although it often appears that children recover quickly from emotional shocks, most children simply repress those feelings that they fear and do not understand; then they express them later in aberrant behavior.

---

[1] U.S. Dept. If Commerce, Bureau of the Census

Parents Need to Understand Children's Reactions to Divorce

For this reason, it is important for you as a parent who has experienced divorce, or who may be considering divorce, to learn as much as possible about the cause and pattern of your child's reaction to the trauma of divorce, and to understand what you can do to lessen the depth and duration of your child's emotional response. For next to the loss of a parent by death, the loss of a father or mother by divorce creates a crisis of family transition that produces the most painful distress your child will ever experience.

Children's Symptoms of Divorce Bereavement

Although the symptoms of divorce bereavement in children can vary from child to child and from family to family, the principal causes remain constant. They include the following, more or less in this order of importance:

1. Loss of the first and most important sanctuary: the family unit.

2. A move from a familiar home, neighborhood, or city to a new environment.

3. The loss of daily contact with a parent.

4. The disruptions of friendships.

5. Financial fears relating to security.

6. Fear that a parent who left Daddy or Mommy also could abandon him.

7. Feelings of guilt by younger children, who perceive that their behavior has driven Daddy or Mommy away.

8. Feelings of shame and embarrassment, which are most acute in teenage children.

9. Fear of an unknown future.

10. Fear of coming home to an empty house or apartment (when the parent with custody works away from the home).

If your child's symptoms of grief include any or all of these causes, they will manifest in various ways, among which the following are most likely to appear according to the age of your child:

Younger Children

Nervousness
Uncontrollable rages
Frequent sickness
Accident proneness
Antisocial behavior
Rebellious behavior
Hyperactivity
Nightmares
Depression

Older Children

Difficulty in concentrating
Forgetfulness
Poor schoolwork
Insomnia
Reclusiveness or social withdrawal
Antisocial behavior
Destructive behavior
Resentment of authority
Over-dependence
Resistance to discipline
Frequent sickness
Accident proneness
Overeating
Truancy
Experimentation with drugs and/or alcohol

Depression
Secretiveness
Sexual promiscuity
Staying away or running away from home
Talk of or attempted suicide

Of all the behavioral changes children can experience, the most predictable response to loss is depression. Normally, the depression of bereavement in children will disappear within a reasonable period of time, and will reflect your own period of grieving. If it continues beyond this time span, depression can be a warning of more serious emotional disturbance, and your child should be evaluated by a mental health practitioner.

As it is with your own bereavement, time usually will greatly modify the manifestation of your child's symptoms. However, if your child is beyond the so-called age of reason (six years), his recollections of the traumas associated with divorce will remain at a subconscious level, available to intrude on his emotional health long beyond the time when he has ceased to express his feelings openly. Therefore, it is important to your child's emotional stability that you do everything possible to help him overcome his secret fears and anxieties.

Techniques for Reducing Your Child's Bereavement Stress

Among the things you can do to help your child recover from the shock of a changed family unit are the suggestions that follow:

1. Let your child know that your family relationships have not been terminated, but have simply changed their form.

2. Stress to your child that you and your divorced partner are his or her parents forever—nothing can change that—and that each parent's love will continue.

3. Seek and exploit opportunities for love of your child to be shared by the other parent, and by all of the grandparents.

4. If possible, avoid uprooting your child from familiar surroundings and friends. Try to stay in the same house or apartment, on the same street. Let your child attend the same school for as long as you are able.

5. If you do move, be careful not to discard any of your child's treasures (books, toys, dolls, etc.).

6. Try to stay as close as possible to the familiar routine of living; avoid changes that affect your child.

7. Recognize your child's basic need for security and consistency, and reinforce these feelings at every opportunity.

8. Give your child time to grieve, and accept and share his or her expressions of grief whenever possible.

9. Encourage your child to share feelings of anger, sadness, and fear with you; and respond to them with reassurance and comfort.

11. Let your child know that he or she was not the cause of your divorce.

11. Don't use your child as a go-between or a weapon in dealing with your former mate.

12. Talk positively to your child about the absent parent; help him to love, understand, and respect him or her. Your child needs to feel secure about the worth of both parents.

13. Spend as much time with your child as possible. If you work and your child has an early bedtime, let him or her stay up longer and sleep later, so you both can share that part of the day.

14. Try not to place an inordinate level of responsibility on your child. Assign reasonable chores, but avoid expressing the idea that he or she now is the one who has to take care of Mommy. This can seriously threaten the child's sense of security.

15. Make possible regular visitation with your child's other parent, and help these visitations to be joyful occasions. Children with limited, uncertain, or no contact with a divorced parent suffer the most severe developmental and emotional distress.

16. Listen, *really* listen to your child when he or she talks to you, and look at him or her during your conversations.

17. Touch and hug your child, hold his or her hand, read to him or her, and in every other way possible give your child reassurance of your love and his or her worth.

18. Avoid taking out your anger and frustration on your child.

19. If he or she is young, arrange for your child to have playmates. If he or she is older, encourage friendships with suitable companions.

20. If your child requires day care, be sure it is a good quality of care. Children can survive quite successfully with a surrogate parent who is warm and loving and responsive.

21. Encourage your child to become appropriately independent.

22. Be aware of any sudden or unusual behavior change in your child that might signify an inordinate level of unresolved stress.

23. On holidays such as Christmas and Thanksgiving, stress that you are a family, and celebrate as a family.

24. Avoid talking about the past with bitterness.

25. Try to look to the future with a positive attitude. Your child will follow your example of coping with courage and confidence.

Stepparenting

Since three out of every five divorced people remarry, usually within three to five years, and since an estimated fifteen million children live at least part-time with stepparents, an important part of dealing with your child's bereavement may involve a new marriage and the expanded stresses it is likely to place on the child. For this reason, it can be of value to you to know in advance some of the emotional hazards of adding a stepparent to your family unit.

Stepparents, like natural parents, bring to marital unions a spectrum of personality configurations, a wide diversity of emotional equipment, and a global difference in environmental backgrounds. Because of these variables in the mental health of stepparents and their mates, it can be inaccurate to generalize about them, for some step-parents bring great happiness to blighted family lives, while others bring emotional chaos.

Nonetheless, there are problems involved with step-parenting that are common to many of the revised family structures resulting from second marriages. Those most frequently observed appear below.

• Children often resent stepparents, and are jealous of the time and affection they receive from their new mates. Because of this resentment, children frequently have difficulty relating to stepparents.

• Society in general continues to take more of a negative than a positive view toward stepparents. This has an inhibiting effect on their acceptance by children.

• A family is the wellspring for emotional support. When the structure of the family changes by the addition of a new adult acting in a parental role, the emotional security of the child can be adversely affected.

• Stepfamilies often are beset by jealousies and conflicts of loyalty, which usually are absent in natural families.

• Relationships in a natural family evolve and develop slowly, whereas a stepparent usually becomes a part of the family in one day, by virtue of a marriage service. Thus, the ties of family are impromptu at best; and the relationship between children and stepparent is without the fixed guidelines of habit.

• When stepparents join a family unit, conflict with children is always close to the surface. The development of successful family relationships requires a high level of stability, emotional maturity, patience, self-control, and objectivity on the part of the natural parent as well as the stepparent.

• When natural parents live in the same community as the stepparent, the role of stepparent is confusing to children, and often in conflict with their feelings.

• Where children have regular visitation with a natural parent, conflicts can arise over the difference between the rules and discipline formerly exercised by the biological parent and those established or enforced by the stepparent. All family structures being unique, it is pretentious and dangerous to offer suggestions for improving family relationships without knowing their nature and the dynamics that may have impaired them. However, having listed problems commonly found in stepfamilies, it may be helpful to propose some ideas for your consideration in dealing with your new role in a family unit that is about to be changed, or has already been changed, by the addition of a stepparent.

Suggestions For Improving Step-parenting Skills

1. If you are now planning to become a stepparent in an existing family, begin to make friends with your future stepchildren as soon as possible. When references to your future role are appropriate, do not say, "I'm going to be your new Mommy (or Daddy)." Instead, say "I want to be a part of your family." This will help reduce the inevitable tensions in your relationship with your soon-to-be stepchildren. It also will reassure them that their identity as a family unit will be expanded rather than impaired.

2. Partners-to-be in many second marriages frequently encounter stress involving money, which often is related to the payment of child support and alimony. If this condition exists for you, it is important to face and discuss the financial implications of other legal and moral obligations and their potential impact on the proposed union.

3. If your wedding has not taken place, involve the children in its planning; allow them to participate in every way possible.

4. If very young children are involved, postpone your honeymoon until they feel most comfortable with the new family structure. Or, if you already have made friends with them and want to be a hero, take them along on your wedding trip; let them know it is a collective honeymoon, in which a new life will be shared by all.

5. Make friends with your new family by spending time with each child *individually*, and with all children as a group, several times a week. Use this time to listen and respond to feelings, and to share a game or hobby you can enjoy collectively. This is letting the child enter into your world at his own pace.

6. Move slowly into the role of surrogate parent. Be supportive of existing standards of discipline, and avoid making changes in these rules until you have been accepted as a member of the family unit.

7. Try not to force your relationships. Readjustment takes time. Accept the fact that you cannot replace the missing parent, and just be yourself.

8. If a new family unit is being formed, it is advisable to move into another house or apartment in the same neighborhood. This will maintain continuity of environment, but will avoid the feeling and expression by the children that "this is *our* house, not yours!" Also, if possible, allow the children to help choose the new place of residence. This will help them to feel a sense of identity with the new family unit.

9. Avoid changes in routine whenever possible, but be open to requests for changes made by the children.

10. Establish and hold routine family meetings on a periodic basis to discuss and resolve problems, and to make or adjust family plans and rules for behavior.

11. Give your partner unquestioned support in the administration of punishment or reprimand; never countermand the request of a natural parent. If you disagree with what is being done, do so after the fact and in private.

12. If both parents bring children to the new union, there is bound to be friction. Expect it, accept it, and work in concert—with the children—to resolve it.

13. In all cases where two families are joined, a certain amount of favoritism is unavoidable. Be on guard against it, and try to avoid it whenever possible.

14. If unresolved and serious conflicts occur in stepfamilies, consider using a local resource for family therapy, in which all members of the family can become involved.

15. As in natural families, most stepfamilies experience personality clashes. For a booklet on how to ease this adjustment, write for "Yours, Mine, Ours" to the Consumer Information Center, Dept. 108G, Pueblo, Colorado 81009.

When night falls, the day's work is ended, the children are in bed, and you contemplate with fear and anxiety the long years of potential periodic conflict that lie ahead, be consoled by this thought: the presence of two biological parents in the home is not nearly as important as the presence of two loving adults who present a strong and positive parent image, and who set an example of successful interaction between a man and a woman engaged in life's most challenging role—the raising of a family.

6
Putting Your Life Back Together

Finding Out What and Who You Are

Unless you happen to be one of the ever-growing-number of women whose early lives were vocation-directed, you were programmed in childhood to be dependent and non-aggressive, to marry and be taken care of by a man, and to find your fulfillment in serving him in the various roles married women play: wife, mother, mistress, servant, companion. With the ending of these roles through death or divorce, your identity as a wife has come to an abrupt halt and you are faced with the most critical decision that comes with bereavement: What identity can you now assume?

Many women—especially those who have been widowed in mid-life or later—are secure financially. For them, the focus toward fulfillment need not be vocational, unless by choice. A much smaller number of women whose bereavement has followed divorce at an earlier age have adequate financial resources, and can elect to remain apart from the work force. However, even for these two groups of women for whom having enough money is not an issue, the basic question must be answered: "*Who* am I? To my parents, I was a daughter; to my husband, I was a wife; to my children, I was a mother. But underneath these roles I have played, *what* and *who* am I really?"

In order to find out who you really are, and what you really want from life, it is necessary to get in touch with your inner self—for there and there only can the answers be found. Today there are a variety of techniques advanced as those that lead to self-knowledge, among them the art of meditation and the discipline of Yoga. And although both these ancient forms of mind and body enrichment have brought many to the end of their search, the Eastern way is not for all. If, in your judgment, they are not for you, you may find the answers you seek in a simpler way, by examining your daydreams, for it is here, in the inner world of fantasy, that you often can find the key to your ideal vocation. Daydreams are expressions of your inner voice, or intuition, and can provide startlingly clear insight into your secret ambitions for self-fulfillment.

Regardless of your method of focusing on what it is you wish to do to find and express your personal identity, once the early and worst pain of bereavement has subsided, it is important that your first priority become an interest in learning *how* and *where* your energies can be focused to bring you to the attainment of your goal of self-realization.

Consider Going Back to School

If you are not possessed of a known learning disability, and if your day-dreams have been of a vocational expression that requires specialized education, go back to school. Each year more and more women whose lives have become displaced by choice or fate have returned to graduate school, to college, or even to high school as a means to the end of finding a self-expression that is interesting and rewarding, as well as financially sustaining.

If one of your inhibitions against returning to school concerns the difference between your age and that of your classmates, be reassured that not only will you *not* be embarrassed by the experience, but you will feel stimulated, renewed, younger and more vital. Today you are sure to find students of all age groups, offering a wide selection of potential friends. It is not unusual for older students who have returned to college to form lasting social relationships with fellow students who are younger, as well as with their peers, for a common educational goal is a strong bond that tends to reduce chronological ages to the median age of the group. This results in a level of social homogeneity which will, in effect, help to restore to you the zest of youth you thought you had lost forever.

If there is any valid reason why a return to school is not possible for you, explore any contacts you may have made as a volunteer, doing work you enjoyed without pay. Very often an avocational expression can be turned into a paying job that you could enjoy, in an area of service that would add to your self-esteem.

Changing Your Life's Focus

If you happen to be a woman of middle years, whose bereavement is compounded by menopause and the so-called empty-nest syndrome, it may be comforting to you to know that thousands of American women each year are successfully changing the focus of their lives from husbands and children to self-expression, or self-actualization. In the process, they are finding an antidote to depression and anxiety, and they are discovering new levels of happiness and optimism about the future. In short, they are learning that life can be a series of progressions in which we use change as a catalyst for growth, for though change often is painful, and sometimes involves us in personal crises for which we are totally unprepared, it is only through change that we can find and accept the option to discover our true selves, and to be the selves we were meant to be.

On the practical side, if you have never worked outside your home, and are unable or unwilling to return to school as a bridge to a job which doesn't involve clerical or service work (which are the occupations of 46 percent of all employed women), you will find that interest, aptitude, and skills testing is available to you at most junior and four-year colleges and universities, as well as at centers for continuing education and at private career-counseling firms. If the tests used are comprehensive and properly interpreted, they will be invaluable to you in choosing the vocational field in which you can hope to find your highest level of success and fulfillment.

In addition to these resources, many churches and civic organizations offer career counseling, as does your local CETA office (funded by the federal government, with the full name of *Comprehensive Employment and Training Act*).

Beware of Potential Financial Pitfalls

If you are among the majority of bereaved women who are not totally secure financially, you need to be aware of the economic pitfalls that can await you in your new social or legal state. These comprise various forms of financial discrimination, including denial of a requested level of credit or delay in receiving it, fictional "requirements" for a second or masculine signature on a lease or loan application, and adverse judgments by credit offices concerning the reliability of alimony and child support payments.

In the past several years, many corporations and business firms have begun to issue credit cards in the names of wives as well as husbands. If you possess such cards in your own name, be sure to use them and pay for your charges promptly. However, if no credit was established in your name during your marriage, you will find your husband's charge accounts closed to you; and establishing personal credit should be one of your first goals.

Unless you are possessed of a fixed income of your own, such as a salary or a trust fund, the best way to establish credit is to open a savings account with a local bank and make regular deposits of sums as large as you can afford. After you have built up a reasonable balance in your savings account, apply for a short-term loan (for any real or fictitious purpose), and pay off the loan a few days or weeks *before* it comes due.

The next step is to apply to your bank for a credit card (*Master Card* or *Visa*). When issued, it will carry a credit limit based on the amount of money you previously borrowed and repaid and/or the amount in your savings account. As soon as you receive your credit card, begin to use it. And be sure to pay each monthly bill as soon as it arrives. After six months of this sort of credit activity, you will have established a clear credit record. Your subsequent requests to local stores, national oil companies, etc. will favorably reflect your meticulous payment experience, and you will be well on your way to establishing your personal identity as a person of financial responsibility. But a word of warning: a credit card can be a heady thing. When used properly, to charge things for which you have the money to pay, it is a valuable convenience. When used because you can't afford to pay for the article or service you wish to acquire, it can become a potential danger which can lead to severe financial peril and stress.

Owning Your Own Home

If you are divorced (or widowed) and are not living in a home you own, or in which you have an equity, you will be well advised to consider home ownership as your best hedge against inflation. Your future economic security may hinge on whether you are at the mercy of endless apartment rent increases, or have made yourself safe against further inflation of housing costs.

If the financial logic of owning your own home appeals to you, and you are trapped by the disparity between your current income and the inflated cost of houses, you may wish to consider teaming up with a friend who is in the same position. If, for example, each of you earns $20,000 a year, you can present a joint mortgage application showing a qualifying income of $40,000 and your credit history can be presented jointly. In this way you can become joint owners of a house in which you may wish to live together, or in which your friend has merely made an investment in relation to his or her share of the equity required for the loan approval.

Credit-Risk Criteria

In applying for a mortgage, you will find that in a period of rising mortgage rates, banks are more likely to approve borderline applications. When mortgage rates fall, you need to present a stronger financial position. Although it is commonly believed that the more you earn, the easier it is to obtain a mortgage loan, and the fact is that banks and mortgage companies have criteria that determine your credit risk potential. Among them are these:

1. Gross income
2. Existing debt (versus income)
3. Record of present and past debt payment
4. Length of current employment
5. Savings or other equities (stocks, bonds, IRA accounts, etc.)
6. Net worth (the value of what you own, such as automobiles, boats, furniture, etc.)
7. Your reputation in the community
8. Earning potential (a graduate degree is more promising than a G.E.D.)
9. Value of property to be mortgaged
10. Location of property to be mortgaged

With the advancing liberation of women from various forms of discrimination, you are less likely to be faced today with this sort of business practice. However, if you believe you are being discriminated against because you are the female head of a household, turn for advice and information to your local Department of Citizens' Service and Information (if there is one), the local office of the U.S. Health and Human Services Department, or the Human Rights Advocacy Commission, which is a facility of your state health and rehabilitation service.

Most of us build our lives around a series of milestones that are keyed to timetables such as "after I finish," "after I'm married," "after the children are grown," "after I achieve some financial independence," or "after I retire." If you are confronted with the unexpected crisis of being without a partner, the day has arrived when you must face the need to find the personal meaning of life for you. If you can accept it as an opportunity for self-exploration and self-determination, you will achieve a level of personal freedom beyond your wildest dreams, and you will know the only security worthy of the name: the inner peace and contentment that comes when you learn to know, accept, and express yourself as the unique daughter (or son) of God that you truly are.

Opening the Door to the Future

In summary, the rebuilding of a life is not an easy task; it is doubly hard when your mind and spirit are filled with grief, remorse, anger, and anxiety. That it can be done is testified to by the legion of valiant women who have accepted and achieved the opportunity for personal growth that is contained in all adversity. To help yourself attain this growth, try not to look back, for a backward look is an anchor to the past, and it is in the future only that your personal fulfillment can be found.

In your search for this fulfillment in a time of sorrow, recall the words of Kahlil Gibran, who wrote, "Sadness is a wall between two gardens." As you grow in understanding and acceptance of yourself, so grow the chances that for you, a time may come to love again. To bring it closer, close the door to the past (without in any way forgetting what lies there). When you do, a door to the future will open. As it swings wide, you may find it to be a door much like one through which you walked before; or it may be as different a door as can be conceived. But if it opens in response to your knock, there is always the possibility that it will lead to chambers of the heart where you have not dwelled before; and you may find the fruit of your life ripening in the fullness of time.

7
Can Divorce Be Avoided?

I f you are faced with the possibility of divorce, or have been divorced and are considering another marriage, you may find this chapter of value. Although a cynical lawyer once said that the only way to escape divorce is to abstain from marriage, there *are* clearly identified ways in which you can increase your odds of avoiding divorce.

The Five Successive Stages Leading to Divorce

Before considering them, however, it may be useful to examine the anatomy of divorce. Although relatively easy to obtain today, with no-fault and mutual-consent laws available in nearly all states, divorce is seldom sought in haste and without careful thought. Rather than viewing divorce as an act of severance alone, it is helpful to see divorce for what it actually is: an extended chronological process involving an internal crisis of relationship with one's mate. This process typically passes through five successive stages:

The *first* stage of the divorce process usually is concerned with an intellectual examination of your emotions. In this step, you analyze your feelings, try to define the reasons for your discontent, and you give initial consideration to the many uncertainties involved if you were to make a change. You anticipate the loneliness that would follow separation, and you search for less-threatening solutions to your marital dysfunction.

At this stage, many women choose to avoid the issue by having a child (or another child), by moving to a larger (or different) house or a new neighborhood, by arranging to take a second honeymoon, or by resorting to any one or more of a number of devices designed to reduce the marriage stress, or to postpone acceptance of the disintegrating union.

The *second* stage of the process also is an intellectual one, but on a more profound level, in which the impact of divorce on your family life, your economic and social life, and your public image is carefully considered. At this stage, most women experience strong ambivalence toward their husbands and their marriages.

The *third* step in the process is a dual one, involving both the decision to separate and the actual act of separation. In marriages where the partner who wants the divorce is possessed of a high level of intellectual honesty, objectivity, and self-control, the third step often is repeated one or more times before the legal system becomes involved.

The *fourth* step in of the process concerns the reorganization of your life, and your inevitable struggle to define your separate identity. This stage is made doubly difficult by the lack of clear role models for divorce in our society, with those that do exist being largely negative in nature.

The *fifth* and last step in the process is the redefinition of a family unit with a single custodial head, and the consideration of how you can best present your redefined family unit to others without impairing its acceptance. The fifth step also involves a redefinition of the relationship of the absent parent with your family, and a structuring of your new family as one with both part-time partners involved in decision making concerning the children, or else one in which the custodial parent receives and accepts full responsibility for the new family unit.

Considering Whether a Dysfunctional Marriage Justifies a Divorce

In considering whether or not the dysfunction of your marriage justifies divorce, there are a number of probable results to making a divorce decision with which you should be familiar. If you have children, these results probably will include the following:

• Divorce always creates depression in children, often in those as young as eighteen months. At this age, however, the effect of separation from a parent can be greatly lessened by frequent touching and cuddling your child in love.

• If your child is six years old or younger when your family structure is changed, he likely will experience a loss of trust and confidence which can remain with him throughout life. And if you should be required to leave your home to work, after the divorce, your child will suffer an even deeper and more painful loss.

• If your child is between the ages of six and twelve at the time of your divorce, he will have begun to understand and respond to your reassurance that the new family unit will meet his needs. Nevertheless, he often will feel like a helpless bystander observing a wreck.

• If your non-adult child is still at home when your marriage is dissolved, the chances are high that he will be conditioned to attempt to escape from problems in his own eventual marriage rather than to seek solutions for them, and his chances for a successful partnership of his own probably are seriously impaired.

• At all ages except infancy, children usually are deeply shocked by the divorce of their parents, and they feel that their personal security is threatened. This shock can be greatly lessened by preparing your child for divorce by sharing your decision to end your marriage with him, after it has been made, before you act upon it. However, it is unwise to discuss in great detail your reasons for reaching the decision; it can be very harmful if you use this opportunity to impair your child's image or relationship with his father or mother.

Insights Concerning Matrimonial Stresses Which Lead to Divorce

If you have not yet reached the first stage in the divorce process, but you have felt concern about the continuation of your marriage, it may be useful to review some insights concerning the state of matrimony which may help you understand various tensions and stresses that can lead to a marriage's dissolution. Here are a few of them:

• Most divorces occur when the partners are around the age of thirty. Statistics show that the seventh to tenth years of marriage are a time when both partners are most vulnerable to the impulse to escape from the marriage and its bonds.

• Most marriages experience mid-life crises, usually caused by pressures related to the raising of children, to not having enough money to meet all family needs and some desires, and/or to various vocational problems of the wage earner(s). It is at these times that the second highest number of divorces occur.

• Many middle-aged women experience severe depression and feelings of inner instability associated with menopause. Today, since these psychological and emotional insecurities can be stabilized and controlled chemically, most women can find the relief needed to restore their emotional balance.

• Most men, perhaps as high as 75 percent to 80 percent, experience a mid-life climacteric, or crisis, of their own. This involves an inner struggle to justify the disparity between their life goals and the attainment of them; to reconcile the work they do with their inner longings or deep-seated desires for self-expression; to accept a diminishing sex drive as a physiological experience rather than a psychological threat to their masculine self-image; to accept the emotional and physical withdrawal of their children at the precise time when interest in them as persons finally has begun to manifest; and to look to the future with optimism and equanimity instead of fear of the uncertainties that the last half of life may hold.

• For many men and most women, middle life is a time when the search for personal identity moves from the outside to the inside. Our vision of life takes on new coloration which can affect our emotional responses to our partners. This evolutionary process in a marriage is further complicated by the fact that mid-life is a time when many men finally are able to allow their emotions to surface and be expressed in shared communication, while their wives now are less responsive to their husbands' needs, in their own concern with the development at last of a sense of separateness, or selfhood.

• Due in great part to the new freedoms of thought and action that the women's liberation movement has produced, many women at mid-life are breaking out of long-inhabited domestic cocoons. Coming as they do at the precise time when most men are experiencing strong feelings of futility and lack of fulfillment, these concurrent evolutionary processes are counterproductive to a halcyon union.

• Nearly all women and most men experience chronological changes in attitudes and feelings as part of the process of living. Unless the changes taking place in each partner are similar, the marriage relationship is subject to stresses that are perceived as threatening, and which can lead to divorce or separation.

• All men and women are a combination of masculine and feminine characteristics, with the ideal being a blend of both in each sex. Today, millions of married women are in the process of liberating their aggressive (male) selves, while few men have been willing to explore their female selves. This dichotomy often leads to a level of friction in marriage that can result in divorce.

Knowledge and anticipation of these various threats to the longevity of marriage can be of significant value in overcoming them, as forewarning can help you to accept the changing physical and emotional dynamics of your partner as a part of the process of living a shared life.

In addition, it may be useful to you to realize that all marriages require periodic readjustments; that no marriage contract remains the same, but instead must be re-negotiated in mid-life. Happiness in marriage is not found in the absence of problems, but in the commitment to accept and face these problems together and to work in concert to overcome the inevitable crises which are a part of all marriages.

Sexual Problems as a Source of Matrimonial Stress

A popular concept about marriage seems to be that sexual problems are a principal cause of most marital stress. Although sex is one cause, it often ranks behind money and communication. However, there are certain aspects of sex in marriage which you should consider in your efforts to avoid divorce. They are set forth below:

Sexual problems in marriage often stem from a lack of communication between partners, due to inhibitions against being explicit about sex needs, desires, and fantasies. Only by telling your mate what pleases you can you attain the level of true intimacy on which most successful marriages are based.

Men in their twenties have higher sex drives than their marriage partners in the same age group. However, as they reach middle years, most men experience a drop in libido, while the sex desire of their mates generally becomes more active. As libido in men is closely related to their masculine self-image, the most successful middle-age unions are those in which the female partner handles the problem of a reverse differential in the need for sex with insight, delicacy, and tact, being careful not to make demands that cannot be met.

Vocational and personal psychological problems of either partner can be responsible for the diminishment of sex drive and other sex difficulties in marriage. If you believe such problems exist, it is wise to consider counseling by a qualified practitioner.

A significant weight gain by either partner can result in a marked change in sexual attractiveness. To maintain a satisfactory level of attraction, many women and men whose marriages remain successful take care of their bodies through appropriate diet and regular exercise.

Studies show that for the majority of women, sexual intercourse is an ineffective way to achieve orgasm; they indicate that perhaps only 30 percent succeed. To find sexual satisfaction, many women resort to masturbation, most of them achieving orgasm in this manner. One national study shows that 82 percent of all women find periodic release in this way.

Despite the great stress put on orgasm today, it is not always the most important part of sex for many women, for whom the deepest fulfillment comes only from mutual relating, sharing, and caring.

Couples with a deep and stable emotional relationship usually maintain a consistent level of mutual sex interest and response throughout their marriage. However, it should be kept in mind that interest can be responsive to the feeling of emotional distance that either partner can experience from time to time.

Money Problems as a Source of Marital Stress

Problems in marriage concerning money can be frequent. Although many couples are concerned about their level of income, the amount of money available to a husband and wife is not as important as how it is spent. Care should be taken to curb tendencies to spend a disproportionate amount of income on recreation, pleasure, and frivolous unnecessary purchases. Because of a tendency to over-spend or over-commit to future debt, couples with moderate incomes who have a fixed savings or investment plan, and who live well within their incomes, have a much greater chance for long and happy unions than couples with large incomes that are over-committed.

Where financial decisions are made principally by the husband, trouble is bound to result. Many middle-years marriage breakups can be traced to the slowly building and eventual exploding of a wife's resentment at her lack of control over how the family income is dispersed. If your marriage is one in which money cannot be budgeted adequately, or is controlled entirely by only one partner, counseling about the handling of money can go a long way to save it from faltering and ending in divorce.

The Need for Communication Skills

All marriages can be enriched by increased knowledge and use of communications skills between partners. Among those techniques that can be helpful in building a better relationship with your partner, the following ideas may be of the most value to you:

• Happy and successful marriages do not just happen. They result from a mutual willingness by both partners to work together toward building a life that is truly satisfying for *each* partner.

• An important factor in the attainment of a successful marriage is a willingness on the part of both partners to discuss and agree on the roles each partner will play in the marriage. This often is easier for younger people than for those who have long been exposed to stereotypical masculine and feminine roles as a part of their social environment.

• In order to produce a mutually satisfying life, it is necessary to learn to share yourself with your partner. Successful sharing requires the mutual revealing of your hopes and dreams, your fears and concerns, your joys and sorrows. Above all, it requires that you *listen* to your partner with empathy, respond with an open and caring heart, and attempt to understand and meet his or her needs.

• In your communication with your partner, try to distinguish between issues and problems. Issues can be anything that relates to a marriage, such as changes of any kind—a new job, a new child, a new home. Issues also can involve feelings of dissatisfaction with your partner, or unexpected life events. Issues only become problems when they are not identified as issues, are not faced, and are not resolved.

• In dealing with issues in a marriage, *what* you say to your partner often is less important than *how*, *when*, and even *where* you say it.

• In communicating with your partner, it is important to understand the differences between statements that express your thoughts, and statements which express your feelings. For example, if you say "I think you are upset," this reflects only your judgment or understanding of your partner's actions. However, if you say "I feel threatened when I think you are upset," this reveals to your partner how your interpretation of his or her actions makes you feel.

• Successful communication between partners is based on mutual awareness, which can only come about by attentive listening and observing. It is helpful to give your full attention to your partner when he or she is speaking to you, to maintain eye contact whenever possible, and to be responsive to his revelations of feelings by sharing your own.

• In dealing with your partner, try to avoid confrontation. For example, if your husband is two hours late getting home, instead of exclaiming, "Why didn't you let me know you'd be late?" try "You must have run into an unexpected situation to be so late. Is everything OK?"

• In communicating with your partner, be sure that he or she not only understands what you have said, but also comprehends the meaning behind it. Often this can best be accomplished by repeating your statement and adding a simple definition of your meaning. For example, if your first statement is "I'm ready for bed," your follow-up statement might be "I'm not really that sleepy, but I feel like being loving with you."

• Successful communication with your partner not only involves voice and eye contact, but also includes physical contact. Touching can modify a statement which, without tender physical contact, could be misinterpreted. For example, if a woman is disturbed about something her partner has done (or said), she might say from across the room, "How many times have I asked you not to do (or say) that!" But if she walked over to her partner, put her arms around him, and said "I love you, you big ox! But how many times do I have to ask you not to say (or do) that," the effect of her words has been modified and reinforced at the same time, and she probably has avoided the conflict that would have resulted from her first approach.

Counseling Can Help Relieve Marital Stress

Achieving and maintaining a successful marriage is never easy, and sometimes requires help from others. The French writer Alexander Dumas once offered the opinion that "The bonds of matrimony are so heavy it sometimes takes three to carry them."

There *are* times when it does take three to carry the heavy chains of matrimony. The needed third party sometimes should be a trained counselor, who can serve as a catalyst in helping distressed and dysfunctional marriage partners to understand the causes of their stress, and who can help them modify their attitudes or behavior.

If you believe that your marriage can be helped by counseling, contact your local family service agency, where you will find well-trained and knowledgeable marriage and family counselors who can guide you in understanding your own feelings and responses, and who can help you to bring about favorable changes in your relationship with your mate. However, to be successful, marriage counseling should involve both partners; the unwillingness of your mate to participate could signify a deeper level of psychological stress, which could point to the ultimate need for more skilled and prolonged personal counseling.

In summary, not all marriages can be saved. Some marriage partners and their children would be better off if divorce ensued. But it is safe to say that *most* marriages can be helped and prolonged by the willingness of partners to work in concert to accomplish mutually acceptable goals for their relationship and their lives together.

As Philip Goldberg has written, the Chinese character for crisis is a combination of the words *danger* and *opportunity*.

No better thought could be found to express the elements inherent in the crisis of an unstable marriage—for at worst, it is fraught with unnumbered perils; at best, it presents an opportunity to use the fabric of two lives to weave a tapestry of unparalleled beauty. Although a partnership between a man and a woman is not for all, for most of us life is not worth the candle unless its light can be shared.

8
The Single Life:
Its Joys and Sorrows

The word *single* has different connotations to people in different circumstances. To the unhappily married person, *single* can stand for blessed release from the chains of a difficult marriage. To the well-adjusted, successful, career-oriented woman, *single* can mean freedom to live her own life without interference.

For all who are single, a life lived alone can have advantages as well as disadvantages. Which outweighs the other will depend in great part on the personality and the mental and physical health of the person living alone, as well as on whether the person's decision to live alone is voluntary or involuntary.

Potential Problems
and Perils in Single Living

For those who are not living alone by choice, a single state can lead to problems and perils, as well as terrors, which may include the following:

• A feeling of being stunned, or paralyzed, if you suddenly are forced by circumstances to change from a life of companionship to one in which there is no one to share your problems, help you make decisions, or to care whether you live or die. *Wow. Me.*

• Being sick when you are alone, and having no one to care for you or to give you sympathy.

- There may be social pressure to marry and emotional pressure to couple, especially if you are a woman. *-True .*

- The thought of growing old alone, with no one to care for you in infirmity. *L Lack of Ability to Procreate .*

- If you are a woman who works in a relatively low-level job, the responsibility of meeting your own living expenses and financial obligations.

- For single women, the potential trap of multiple sex encounters that can lead to unwanted pregnancy, venereal disease, social disapproval, and lowered self-esteem.

- For all people living alone, an increased incidence of heart attacks, lung cancer, strokes, influenza, and pneumonia.

- For men living alone, cirrhosis of the liver and tuberculosis are likely threats.

- For most single people, the risk of a level of social isolation that can lead to severe emotional stresses. There is a biological basis for the need to form human relationships. When this need is not met, physical deterioration can follow, resulting in generally impaired health. *Man is not meant to be alone.*

The Challenge of
Loneliness and Depression

Of all the trials of a single life, the most universal is loneliness. And although loneliness sometimes is present in marriage, when it results from an unwilling single state, it is far more pervasive and intense. According to the weight of psychiatric authority, loneliness also can result in death. Seen in this light by lay persons as well as professionals in the field of mental health, loneliness is appropriately decried by W. H. Auden, the English poet, when he writes "We must love one another or die." *Mine · When.*

Extensive research concerning loneliness has led James J. Lynch, M.D., of the University of Maryland School of Medicine, to report dialogue with another person as the most essential element in overcoming loneliness. He sees verbal interaction between two people as "the elixir of life itself."

If loneliness is prolonged, depression results, and the process of human deterioration is accelerated. Most severe depressions are related to an extreme lack of human contact, and although ours is a country known the world over for its open, gregarious, and friendly nature, a Gallup Poll of 1980 revealed that 10 percent of our citizens have only one or two friends, and 3 percent have no friends at all.

Removing loneliness and depression from the life of a single person is not always easy, and sometimes is impossible. Nonetheless, these two scourges of mental and physical well-being can be combated with some success by following the suggestions appearing below.

Techniques for Overcoming Loneliness and Depression

For obvious reasons, friendships must be formed; the suggestions advanced in Chapters 2, 3 and 4 of this book can be useful to you in developing social situations from which friendships can flow.

Try to maintain at least one solid, dependable social base in your life. If you have relatives with whom you are compatible, their home can serve this purpose well. Annual or other periodic visits should be made for the purpose of reaffirming your social roots and restoring your sense of identity. If you have no relatives who can meet this need, the home of an old and close friend can serve the same purpose. No matter how far the distance from your friend, it is important that your visits be regular and no less frequent than once a year. The very process of planning and being able to look forward to such visits will go far toward relieving your loneliness and depression.

exercise As loneliness and depression bring responsive physical stress, you can combat them more successfully if you take care to build and maintain a high level of physical energy. This can be done by following a planned exercise program, indoors or out, and steadily increasing the amount of exercise you undertake until your body has responded with a new vitality. You also can improve your physical condition by eating three times a day (only), and by avoiding or cutting down on your use of coffee, cigarettes, stimulants, tranquilizers, and alcohol (which will bring you early relaxation, but later depression; and when used to excess at night, nearly always results in early-morning wakefulness).

If you happen to be plagued by insomnia (as most lonely *True.* and depressed people are), this program of exercise and controlled diet is sure to help you to experience longer and deeper sleep.

— *Yes!*

Night-time is known to be the most successful enemy of a tranquil spirit in those who live alone, and it deserves special consideration. To overcome the loneliness which comes in the dark and quiet of the night, make your bedroom (or your bed) a pleasant place to use as your retreat. Be sure that your sleeping needs are as well met as possible, and that you have a good reading light, an interesting book, a radio, a clock and a flashlight by your bed. When sleep won't come, for whatever reason, and you are bored with reading, get up and accomplish some special task you have been putting off. Not only will this effort expend physical and emotional energy, but the virtuous feeling that comes from completing a task you have been avoiding will give you a feeling of euphoria, which is easily transferred into restful slumber.

If your efforts to combat loneliness and depression are unsuccessful at any point, and if you feel like you will explode from anxiety, call your local hot line or crisis center for instant telephone contact with another person who has volunteered to receive, listen, and respond to the calls of lonely people in distress.

The Advantages of a Single Life

According to a 1980 Gallup survey, 74 percent of American women will choose marriage and children over a single life. However, for those who prefer to be single, or who find an unexpected solo act to be to their liking, the advantages most often mentioned by women living alone are these:

• Pride in directing your own life, in being in control of yourself and your destiny, in making your own decisions without a hassle, and in coping with life successfully.

• Although loneliness can impair happiness as a single person, living alone is infinitely preferable to being caught in an unhappy marital relationship.

• The freedom from being responsible for the contentment of another person; the lack of pressure to have to please someone else or to pay a penalty for not doing so.

• The excitement of being free to move in any social direction you choose, without criticism or obstruction.

• The opportunity to form an infinite number of social relationships without impairing any one of them; the freedom from possessive jealousy.

• The freedom to live at your own pace, in a place of your own choosing, sleeping and eating when you please.

• Freedom to focus your energies on a fulfilling and rewarding career, without restrictive obligations to another person.

• Freedom to visit friends of your choice, when you wish, without regard to the prejudices, likes, and dislikes of another.

• Freedom to accept travel invitations; the excitement of making your own travel decisions and experiencing travel uninhibited by the needs, desires, and prejudices of another.

• Freedom to live as you please; to be dressed or undressed as you wish; to be neat or slovenly, as the spirit moves; to be hot or cold, without regard for the comfort of anyone else.

• Freedom to listen to music of your choice, when and for as long as you wish to hear it. Freedom to furnish and decorate your home to your own taste, without compromise with another.

• Freedom from incurring the expense of raising children, as shown below in a 1995 table* of child-rearing costs:

Cost of Raising a Child from Birth to Age 17

$178,000	$241,440	$350,920
Annual family income less than $33,000	Annual family income from $34,000 to $58,000	Annual family income $58,000 and above

Certainly, the single life is not for everyone. Statistics show that 95% of all Americans have been married or will marry at some point in their lives.

But there are many, who at least for a significant interlude in their lives, find that being single has sufficient and significant advantages that they choose it as their preferred status. They truly find real contentment in the many freedoms which it gives to them, and enjoy peace, happiness, success and contentment as they live the single lifestyle.

Epilogue

Body, Mind and spirit

All men and women are endowed with three elements: body, mind and spirit. To function well, these elements must be in balance. This insight is shared by most thoughtful people. Although mental needs are fulfilled by various levels of educational activities for the mind, and physical needs are met with food and exercise for the body, one's spiritual needs are sometimes put on hold until ill health, a serious accident, or some kind of life trauma causes the mind to give forceful recognition to the third element.

Small children, when permitted to develop their thought processes without suggestive or dogmatic influence, have a clear perception of their spiritual element. And unless this process in interrupted, they form a firm bond with their spiritual natures that lasts until parent or peer-group influence replaces intuition. At some point in later life, the fortunate child will recall his intuitive link with his spirituality. Given the freedom to avoid the time constraints that inhibit reflection, he begins a solitary communication with the spirit within. When this occurs, recognition comes of the power of the spirit to nurture, enlighten and heal; and a beginning is made toward attainment of a balance of the three elements with which we are endowed.

The Value of Meditation, Contemplation and Prayer

If you have searched in vain, in a bereaved state, for a sustaining force, it can be found in solitary contemplation when the mind is open to receive long-buried insights and new inspirations, when meditation and silent prayer call forth strengths that lie in subconscious recesses of the mind, and when childhood recollections of an inner life can be transmuted into perceived reality. At this point, and not before, true healing of a wounded heart can begin.

If you have difficulty in getting in touch with the spiritual side of your nature, the discipline of daily meditation has been found to be of value in replacing the cares of the day with a feeling of peace that allows the mind to become still. Accumulated stress begins to dissolve.

Introduced to the Western world in 1965 at the Harvard Business School by the Maharishi Masesh Yogi in a series of lectures, the Eastern discipline of meditation was found by Harvard physicians and medical students in attendance to reduce the rate and depth of respiration and quiet the mind, a result predicted by the Maharishi, who likened the mind to a monkey leaping from limb to limb, that could be quieted in meditation by silently focusing on a word, form, or sound of choice.

If this mental exercise appeals to you, it can be done for fifteen minutes every morning before breakfast, and every evening before dinner, or at bedtime. If you are tired after a busy day and fall asleep during your quiet time of meditation, you will feel relaxed when you awaken, and you will know that the pressures that caused your stress have been attacked where they appeared, in your mind.

During the years since the Maharishi's first visit to America's shores, the relaxing technique of meditation has received scientific approval as a discipline that can reduce stress; and many medical and social scientists believe that when the mind is in a receptive state, the body can receive healing from within.

This is the message that I would leave with you: if and when the darkness of grief threatens to overcome you, let your thoughts turn within in meditation and prayer, for there alone will you find the true healing light of your own being and of your communication with the Divine.

Bibliography

Grief and Bereavement Resulting From Death

Books

Bova, Ben and Barbara Berson. *Survival Guide for the Suddenly Single*. New York: St. Martin's Press, 1974.

Bozarth, Alla Renee. *A Journey Through Grief.* Center City, MN: Hazeldon Foundation 1990.

Brothers, Dr. Joyce. *Widowed.* New York: Ballantine Books, Inc., 1991.

Childs-Gowell, Elaine. *Good Grief Rituals: Tools for Healing.* Barrytown, NY: Station Hill, 1992.

Feinberg, Linda. *I'm Grieving As Fast As I Can: How Young Widows and Widowers Can Cope and Heal.* Dallas TX: New Horizon, 1994.

Fitzgerald, Helen. *The Mourning Handbook: Comprehensive Resource Offering Practical and Compassionate Advice on Coping With All Aspects of Death and Dying.* New York: Simon & Schuster, 1995.

Fitzgerald, Helen. *A Complete Guide for the Bereaved.* New York: Simon & Schuster, 1997.

Ginsberg, Genevieve Davis. *Widow to Widow.* Tucson AZ: Fisher Books, 1998.

Glick, Ira O., Robert Weiss and Murray Parkes. *The First Year of Bereavement*. New York: John Wiley & Sons, 1974.

Grollman, Earl A. *Living When a Loved One Has Died*, 3rd Edition. Boston: Beacon Press, 1994.

Hickman, Martha. *Healing After Loss: Daily Meditations for Working Through Grief*. New York: Avon Books, 1994.

James, John W. and Russell Friedman. *The Grief Recovery Handbook: The Action Program for Moving Beyond Death, Divorce and Other Losses*. New York: Harper Collins Publishers, Inc., 1998.

Jowell, Barbara and Donette Schwisow. *After He's Gone: A Guide for Widowed and Divorced Women*. Secaucus, NJ: Carol Publishing Group, 1997.

Kastenbaum, Robert J. *The Psychology of Death*, 2nd Edition. New York: Springer Publications, 1992.

Kratzler, Mel: *Learning to Love Again*. New York: Harper Collins Publishing, Inc. 1987.

Larson, Hal and Susan Larson. *Suddenly Single!: A Lifeline for Anyone Who Has Lost a Love*. San Francisco: Halo Books, 1993.

Levy, Naomi. *To Begin Again: A Journey Toward Comfort, Strength and Faith in Difficult Times*. New York: Alfred A. Knopf, Inc., 1998.

Lewis, C. S. *A Grief Observed*. New York: Bantam Books, Inc., 1976.

Mellonie, Bryan and Robert Ingpen. *Lifetimes: A Beautiful Way to Explain Death to Children*. New York: Bantam books, Inc., 1983.

Parkes, Collin Murray and Robert S. Weiss. *The First Year of Bereavement*. New York: John Wiley & Sons, 1974.

Rando, Therese: *How to Go On Living When Someone You Love Dies.* New York: Bantam Books, Inc., 1991.

Sanders, Catherine M. *Surviving Grief: And Learning to Live Again.* New York: John Wiley & Sons, Inc., 1992.

Sittser, Gerald L. and John Smith. *A Grace Disguised.* Grand Rapids, MI: Zondervan Publishing House, 1998.

Staudacher, Carol. *Beyond Grief: A Guide for Recovering From the Death of a Loved One.* Oakland, CA: New Harbinger Pub., 1987.

Staudacher, Carol. *A Time To Grieve: Meditations for Healing After the Death of a Loved One.* San Francisco; Harper, 1994.

Sherokee, Ilse and Elizabeth Levang. *Remembering With Love: Messages Of Hope For The First Year Of Grieving And Beyond.* Minneapolis: Fairview Press, 1995.

Tatelbaum, Judy. *The Courage to Grieve: Creative Living, Recovery and Growth Through Grief.* New York: Harper Collins Publishers, Inc., 1984.

Wanderer, Zev and Tracy Cabot. *Letting Go: A 12 Week Personal Action Program to Overcome a Broken Heart.* New York: Dell Publishing Co., Inc., 1987.

Wannamaker, Catherine. *Suddenly Alone.* Sarasota, FL: Equity Ent., 1998.

Zandra, Dan. *Forever Remembered.* Edmonds, WA: Compendium Press, 1997.

Ziglar, Zig. *Confessions of a Grieving Christian.* Thomas Nelson Publishers, 1998.

Articles

Blessing, Angela. "Memories of love make a spouse's death both more heartbreaking and, in the end, more bearable." (Joyce Brothers on the death of her husband, Milton Brothers.) *People Weekly*, June 26, 1989, v. 31, n. 25, p. 86(4).

Bower, Bruce. "Grief sometimes heads down a grievous path." (Bereavement-related depression distinguished from complicated grief.) *Science News*, January 14, 1995, v. 147, n. 2, p. 22(1).

Bower, Bruce. "Bereavement: reeling in the years." (A study of the psychological effects of sudden loss of a spouse or child.) *Science News*, February 7, 1987, v. 131, p. 84(1).

Clahan, Sidney. "A mother's death: is this what God demands?"(Column) *Commonweal*, May 17, 1996, v. 123, n. 10, p. 7(2).

Cappel, Mary Lou and Susan Leifer. "Loss and the grieving process." (The death of loved ones.) Mathieu. *Parks & Recreation*, May 1997, v. 32, n. 5, p. 82(4).

Covington, Dennis. "Going it alone." (How various widowers have learned to cope with their loss and grief.) *Redbook*, May 1994, v. 183, n. 1, p. 100(4).

DeMarco, Tony. "After Maureen" (A widowed sportswriter is left alone to raise his 9-year-old daughter.) *People Weekly*, October 13, 1997, v. 48, n. 15, p. 117(3).

Edelman, Hope. "Gone too soon?" (The author of the bestseller 'Motherless Daughters' writes about her own love and loss. Includes a related article on coping.) *Ladies Home Journal*, April 1995, v. 112, n. 4, p. 56(4).

Forsyth, Sondra. "I'm in agony & he doesn't care." (A couple therapy case study; includes related article on being a friend to someone who is grieving.) *Mademoiselle*, November 1996, v. 102, p. 3(3). Fiche Coll.: 85M2176. n. 11, p. 17.

Goodman, Susan. "Coming to terms with death." (Includes related articles.) *Current Health,* 2 March 1988, v. 14, n. 7, p. 3(6).

Gould, Meredith. "Handling bereavement." (Mourning death in the workplace.) (To Your Health) *Nation's Business*, August 1995, v. 83, n. 8, p. 61(l).

Gromer, Crystal. "An etiquette for grief: How to help others go through a loss." *Reader's Digest*, March 1998, v. 152, n. 911, p. 79(3).

Hunter, Dorothy. "Something in God; in the desert." (Column). *The Christian Century*, July 28, 1993, v. 10, n. 22, p. 734(2).

Kantrowitz, Barbara. "Beyond the tears." (Figure skater Ekaterina Gordeeva.) *People Weekly*, March 25, 1996, v. 45, n. 12, p. 78(8).

Kort, Michele. "How a man mends his broken heart." (Actor Pierce Brosnan copes with his wife's death.) (Interview) *Redbook*, December 1995, v. 186, n. 2, p. 63(2).

Lamott, Anne. "Have a good cry: when my best friend died, I finally learned that there was only one way to begin to heal." (Column) *Ladies Home Journal*, May 1995, v. 112, n. 5, p. 218(l).

Lightner, Candy and Nancy Hathaway. "The other side of sorrow." (Grieving after the loss of a loved one.) *Ladies Home Journal*, September 1990, v. 107, n. 9, p. 158(4).

Lipstein, Owen and Hara Marano. "Loss." (An interview with Froma Walsh.) *Psychology Today*, July-August 1992, v. 25, n. 4, p. 64(9).

Lord, Mary. "Finding a way to grieve." (Spontaneous memorials to victims of tragedies.) *U.S. News & World Report*, July 28, 1997, v. 123, n. 4, p. 16(1).

Myers, Ed. "When someone you love dies." (How survivors react to loss.) *Glamour*, November 1986, v. 84, p. 284(3).

Perry, Collin. "Help yourself through the hard times." *Reader's Digest*, February 1997, v. 150, n. 898, p. 123(4).

Putnam, Nicholas. "Conversations with Ariane." (A father faces difficult questions when a three-year-old learns of the death of her mother. Includes bibliography of books dealing with death.) *Parents' Magazine*, August 1985, v. 60, p. 72(b).

Rodale, Ardath and Sharon Stocker. "Beyond grief: a guide to reconciling life after loss." (Includes a related article on one person's experience, and a list of support agencies to help people deal with their grief.) *Prevention*, August 1994, v. 46, n. 8, p. 88(9).

Rodale, Ardath. "Climbing toward the light." (Excerpt) *Good Housekeeping*, January 1990, v. 210, n. 1, p. 152(2).

Rosemond, John. "When children grieve: helping them cope with the pain." *Better Homes and Gardens*, August 1988, v. 66, n. 8, p. 26(2).

Steinbach, Alice "A shoulder to cry on." (Grief therapists.) *Redbook* July 1993, v. 181, n. 3, p. 43(3).

Tarpley, Natasha. "Yearning for daddy." (A child's grief after her father dies.) (Column) *Essence*, November 1994, v. 25, n. 7, p. 54(1).

Thompson, Catherine and Barbara E. Moore. "Grief is not a sign of weakness." (Changes in society affect views on psychological state.) *USA Today* (Magazine), July 1991, v. 120, n. 2554, p. 92(2).

Wall, James M. "On the triumph of memories." (About Will Rogers) (editorial) *The Christian Century,* October 11, 1989, v. 106, n. 29, p. 899(2).

"Grief should not be suppressed." *USA Today* (Ed.) (Magazine), April 1994, v. 122, n. 2587, p. 11(l).

"Changing attitudes toward death and dying." *USA Today* (Ed.) (Magazine), April 1994, v. 122, n. 2587, p. 16(l).

"Grief is no killer." (Dying of a broken heart is re-examined.) (Ed.) *Time,* September 5, 1988, v. 132, n. 10, p. 55(l).

"Erroneous assumptions about bereavement." *USA Today* (Ed.) (Magazine), December 1986, v. 115, p. 5(l).

Grief and Bereavement Resulting From Divorce

Books

Ahrons, C., Ph.D. *A Good Divorce: Keeping Your Family Together When Your Marriage Comes Apart.* New York: Harper Collins Publishers, Inc., 1995.

Bova, Ben and Barbara Benson. *Survival Guide for the Suddenly Single.* New York: St. Martin's Press, 1974.

Clapp, Genevieve. *Divorce and New Beginnings: An Authoritative Guide to Recovery and Growth. Solo Parenting and Stepfamilies.* New York: John Wiley & Sons, 1992.

Edwards, Marie and Eleanor Hoover, *The Challenge of Being Single.* New York: Hawthorne, 1974.

Fisher, Bruce. Rebuilding: *When Your Relationship Ends.* New York: Impact Publishing, Inc., 1998.

Fisher, Esther O. (Ed). *Impact of Divorce on the Extended Family.* New York: Hayworth Press Inc., 1982.

Gray, John, Ph.D. *Mars and Venus: Starting Over: A Practical Guide for Finding Love Again After a Painful Breakup, Divorce or the Loss of a Loved One.* New York: Harper Audio, 1998.

Hannon, Kerry. *Suddenly Single: Money Skills for Divorcees and Widows.* New York: John Wiley & Sons, Inc., 1998.

Hirsch, Barbara B. *Divorce: What a Woman Needs to Know.* Chicago: Henry Regnery Co., 1975.

Trafford, Abigail. *Crazy Time: Surviving Divorce and Building a New Life.* New York: Harper Collins Publishers, Inc., 1992.

Wegscheider-Cruse, Sharon. *Life After Divorce: Create a New Beginning.* Metuchen, NJ: Health Communications, Inc., 1993.

Index

About The Author

During his eight years at The Gunston School, on Maryland's Eastern Shore, Keith Hafer aspired to be an army officer, like his father during the first world war. Later, while a boarding student at The Haverford School in Philadelphia, his vocational interests included writing, teaching and diplomacy. After graduating from George Washington University Law School in the nation's capital, he attained all four ambitions—as an Infantry Officer in the U.S. Army, a U.S. Foreign Service Officer at the American Embassy in Paris, an advertising executive with N.W. Ayer & Son on the east and west coasts, and as a member of the faculties of the Universities of Virginia, Georgia, Texas and Puerto Rico.

While following his various vocations, Dr. Hafer was active in social work as Founder and President of the Family Service Association of Bucks County, Pennsylvania; Director of the Family Service Association of America in New York City; director of Family Service of Santa Monica, California; and a member of the Board of Trustees of the Family Service Association of Greater Boston, Massachusetts.

In 1968, deciding to acquire academic credentials in counseling, he studied psychology at Harvard and New York Universities and the University of Virginia, serving a two-year internship as a Marriage and Family Counselor at Family Service of Norfolk, Virginia. In 1974, he was licensed as a Professional, and entered private practice as a Marriage and Family Counselor in St. Petersburg, Florida. Now retired, Dr. Hafer resides in Chambersburg, Pennsylvania with his wife, who continues to practice as a marriage and Family Counselor.